THE ALCHEMIST'S
SECRET

ISABEL CECILIA WILLIAMS

1st WORLD
LIBRARY
Literary Society

The Alchemist's Secret

Isabel Cecilia Williams

© 1st World Library, 2006
PO Box 2211
Fairfield, IA 52556
www.1stworldlibrary.com
First Edition

LCCN: 2006935236

Softcover ISBN: 1-4218-2489-2
Hardcover ISBN: 1-4218-2389-6
eBook ISBN: 1-4218-2589-9

Purchase *"The Alchemist's Secret"*
as a traditional bound book at:
www.1stWorldLibrary.com/purchase.asp?ISBN=1-4218-2489-2

1st World Library is a literary, educational organization
dedicated to:

- Creating a free internet library of downloadable ebooks

- Hosting writing competitions and offering book
publishing scholarships.

Interested in more 1st World Library books?
contact: literacy@1stworldlibrary.com
Check us out at: www.1stworldlibrary.com

1ˢᵗ World Library Literary Society

Giving Back to the World

"If you want to work on the core problem, it's early school literacy."

> — **James Barksdale, former CEO of Netscape**

"No skill is more crucial to the future of a child, or to a democratic and prosperous society, than literacy."

> — **Los Angeles Times**

Literacy... means far more than learning how to read and write... The aim is to transmit... knowledge and promote social participation."

> — **UNESCO**

"Literacy is not a luxury, it is a right and a responsibility. If our world is to meet the challenges of the twenty-first century we must harness the energy and creativity of all our citizens."

> — **President Bill Clinton**

"Parents should be encouraged to read to their children, and teachers should be equipped with all available techniques for teaching literacy, so the varying needs and capacities of individual kids can be taken into account."

> — **Hugh Mackay**

CONTENTS

THE PASSING OF TONY

"Last mail in, Mis' Bascomb?"

"Last mail's in, Tony."

"Be there anything for me to-night?"

Widow Bascomb knew perfectly well there was not, but she reached for a small pile of letters in a pigeonhole on her right and glanced over them rapidly. Her sour visage and rasping voice softened perceptibly as she smiled on the little old man before her.

"Sorry, Tony, there's nothing for you to-night."

"Thank you, Mis' Bascomb, p'raps it'll come to-morrow," and Tony turned away with a sigh and moved towards the door.

A group of men were gathered around the stove, smoking and exchanging the gossip of the town. These greeted him kindly as he passed and he returned the greetings half absently. Before opening the door, the old man stopped to give his woolen muffler one more turn around his neck.

"Purty cold snap, this," he remarked to the company in general. "Looks as if we'd have snow 'fore mornin' and a white Christmas after all. Good-night, Mis' Bascomb; good-night boys. A merry Christmas to you all!" and Tony stepped out into the frosty air of the December evening.

He sighed again as he turned up over the hill to the left and started for home. It had been a long, cold walk down to the village, and it would be equally long and even colder on the way back, for a sharp wind was blowing directly in his face. It was a bad night for an old man like Tony to be abroad and he was almost sorry that he had ventured out. But there was his promise to Martha; it would never do to break that. Martha had always been of a more hopeful turn of mind than he, anyway. While she was still alive she had imparted to him the same spirit of trust and hopefulness which shone in her steady gray eyes, but since God had taken Martha and left him all alone in the world of care and trouble, life had been hard indeed.

He had promised Martha never to omit the daily visit to the post-office to inquire for the letter which, thus far, had failed to arrive. Martha had been so sure that Sallie would write to them some day; Sallie, their handsome, wilful daughter, who had passed out of their lives nearly fifteen years before. He never blamed Sallie for wanting to leave them; what could a tiny village like this offer to one as clever, as pretty, as ambitious as Sallie had been? The neighbors had said many unkind things of Sallie but he heeded them not. They had called her vain, idle and silly; they said the folks at the big house had spoiled her and put notions into her head. They told him he did a foolish thing when he allowed her to go as maid to the lady of the big house over on the shores of the lake, and to go down to the city with the family when they moved home in the autumn. To tell the truth, poor Tony had little voice in the matter. Sallie, as usual, had taken affairs into her own hands and decided for herself.

Nearly fifteen years! It was a long, long time; and never a word from the truant since the day she had left the village. Martha had waited, at first impatiently, then anxiously, and finally with a pathetic hopefulness that was more than half assumed. It was she who had insisted that Tony must go to the office every day, and during those long years, every evening, rain or shine, the same little scene was enacted in the village post-office. Every evening he had the same story of failure to report.

"No letter to-night, mother."

"Never mind, father; it'll sure come to-morrow," and Martha would sigh and clasp her hands in her lap.

Presently, by the movement of her lips he would know she was praying for the absent one. He would lay aside his pipe, fetch his beads, and together they would say the Rosary, begging the blessed Mother of God to keep special watch over their child. She was the only one they had left, four little white stones marking the resting-place of the four little angels who had been permitted to remain with them for only such a very short space of time.

Martha was sleeping now beside her babies and he was alone in the world; for who could tell what had become of Sallie? She, too, might be at rest in God's Acre. Sometimes he felt that she must be, or surely, surely, some word would have come from her. She must have known how anxiously they would watch for news of her, and certainly she would not be so heartless as to keep silence all this long time.

Perhaps she had written and the letter failed to reach them. Well, whatever the trouble was, Tony had long since given up all hope of hearing from her, but, because of his promise to Martha, he still made his nightly visit to the post-office in the village. Had it not been for that promise he would certainly not take that long walk day after day, in summer heat and winter storms, for hope had long since died in Tony's heart. At least, so he told himself, but somehow the walk home always seemed twice as long as the walk down, after hearing those depressing words "No letter to-night, Tony."

Of late, the daily visit to the village had been almost more than the old man's failing strength had been able to support. How often he wished he had not been obliged to sell Lassie. She was the last of his horses to go; the last, in fact, of all his possessions. There was nothing left to him now but the old house, and that was in such a state of dilapidation as to be really unfit for habitation. In the old days, his dogs and his horses were better housed than he was now; in the old days, when his farm was one of the most prosperous in that section of the country. It was lonely indeed since Martha went away, but he was glad she had not lived to see him brought to this pass. He was glad he had been able to surround her with comforts up to the very end, though to do so he had been obliged to sell timber-land, horses, cows, everything he owned, one after another.

But Martha never knew; patient, suffering Martha, confined to her room by illness for many years before God had sent her release from pain. Thank God, Martha never knew; she had trouble enough without worrying over their poverty. Her room was always bright, always cheerful; her favorite flowers blossomed in the window, a fire of logs burned cosily upon the hearth. The neighbors were kind in helping him to care for her, in bringing her little delicacies to tempt an invalid's appetite; fresh eggs, chickens, new lettuce, which Martha supposed had come from their own farm.

It would never do to let her know that all their land was gone, all save that upon which the house stood and Martha's flower garden which stretched from her windows to the road. How he had worked in that garden, cultivating the flowers she loved to see growing there. Sometimes he would lift her from the bed and place her in the large chair by the window, where she could watch him at his work; where she could watch, too, the road that led from the village. Often, he would glance up from his spading to meet her brave, cheery smile that sweetened all his labor; oftener still, it would be to find her eyes fixed upon that long, dusty line that wound over hill and valley, in and out through orchards and corn fields, the road that led to the village and thence to the city beyond. He knew her mind had gone out into the wide, busy world, of which an occasional echo would reach them, gone out in a vain effort to guess at the whereabouts of the girl who had passed down that country road so many years ago never to return. To the very end, Martha had never ceased hoping, never ceased praying for the return of the wanderer, or at least for some word of assurance that all was well with her.

By the time Tony reached the dismantled farmhouse the snow was falling thickly, silently, on all around.

"Twill be a bad storm," thought Tony. "God pity any who are abroad this night."

Pushing open the kitchen door he entered quickly, divesting himself of cap, muffler, and ragged overcoat, and hanging them near the stove to dry. He lighted the lamp and threw some wood upon the fire which had burned low. Then, turning, he spied for the first time, a basket upon the table. A pleased smile overspread his face. So they had not forgotten, after all! How he and Martha had always watched for that Christmas basket from Cousin John's folks over at the market town! It was not so much the value of the gift, for John was not over-plentifully blessed with the goods of this world and had a large family dependent upon him. It was more the fact of being remembered kindly, the knowledge that there was still some one who thought of them occasionally.

He commenced unpacking the basket and arranging the contents upon the table: home-baked bread, pies, cakes; a package of tea, another of tobacco; oranges, nuts, candy; warm mittens and socks that John's wife had knit for him. She was a good woman, John's wife, kind-hearted and thoughtful; she must have guessed how badly he needed socks and mittens now that Martha was no longer there to make them for him. He started for the cupboard, a pie in one hand, a loaf of bread in the other, then stopped in the middle of the room and eyed them meditatively. What was it Martha used to say?

"Never, never let Christmas pass without doing something for some one. No matter how poor one may be, Tony, they're always others poorer still. If it be no more'n a loaf of bread, give something to the poor at Christmas time in the name of the little Babe that had none but the shepherds to do a hand's turn for Him."

Each year he and Martha had found some one to whom they gave in the Christ-Child's name, for the sake of the girl who was never absent from their thoughts by day or by night. Even last year, as poor as he was, he had met with one more needy still and sent him on his way rejoicing - a poor lad, out of work, out of money, tramping from city to city in search of employment. They had taken him in for Sallie's sake, given him food and shelter, and when the boy left the farm a silver dollar, nearly the last of Tony's small store, was pressed into his hand. The dollar had been returned, for at the next town the object of Tony's charity had found steady work. That was last year. This Christmas he was not doing a thing for any one; he had forgotten completely, probably because Martha was not there to remind him.

He placed the bread and the pie back upon the table and stood looking at them long and earnestly. He knew of one who needed them far more than he did, a poor widow over in "the hollow," whose five small children, sickly, starved little creatures, were more than half the time crying with cold and hunger. He opened the package of tobacco, filled his pipe and sat down in his chair by the stove to smoke and think.

How those poor children would enjoy the bread and pies and cakes which John's wife had sent him! Poor little things, they seldom, if ever, tasted fare like that. He really did not need them; he managed to get along pretty well and the neighbors were all good to him; especially since Martha died. He would really be glad to give those children something, but he was so tired, so tired, and it was quite a walk over to the hollow.

Then, the storm! How the wind shrieked and tore around the house, and how steadily the snow beat against the window panes! It was warm and comfortable there by the fire, but outside -. And he was unusually tired to-night; that walk to the village had been almost too much for him. Besides, he must be up in time for first Mass in the morning; he had never missed first Mass and Holy Communion on Christmas since the day he and Martha were married. Year after year, they had knelt side by side at God's altar; for many years Sallie had knelt there with him; now he was all alone but he meant to continue the custom for Martha's sake.

How the storm did rage, to be sure; but those poor children, those poor little children! Perhaps somewhere in the wide world his Sallie was in need of help and comfort this night and those who might give it to her were too tired or too lazy. He guessed that was the trouble, he was growing lazy in his old age. Well, he would do this for Sallie; it would be one more little sacrifice added to the many which he and Martha had offered for their wandering child, that God might keep guard over her wherever she might be. Yes, he would do it for Sallie's sake and to please Martha. From Heaven she was watching him and would know that to please her and for the sake of their child he was going to brave the storm once more and carry a little Christmas happiness to those poor children over in the hollow. The walk over and back again would not hurt him; he was growing old and lazy, that was all.

But first he must light the lamp. Dear, dear, he was growing forgetful as well as lazy. He had nearly forgotten to light Sallie's lamp. What would Martha say to that? Every night as soon as dusk had fallen, Martha had insisted upon placing a lamp in the window of what had once been Sallie's room. If the child came back unexpectedly, she would see the light shining from her window and know they were waiting and watching for her. The room itself was as she had left it years ago, her clothes still hanging in the closet, her slippers laid ready for the tired feet to slip into them, the fire on the hearth all prepared against the day of her home-coming, and by night the lamp in the window shining a welcome that could be seen afar down the road that led from the village. He must light Sallie's lamp, then off once more into the storm and darkness to carry a bit of Christmas cheer to the little home in the hollow.

Nearly an hour later, a thoroughly worn-out but very happy old man sat by the stove in the farmhouse kitchen. He was too tired even to light his pipe; he simply sat there and tried to rest. It had been a hard fight against the storm, but how pleased those poor little children were! Well, he had done it for Sallie, just one more little sacrifice for Sallie who was somewhere out there in the cold, weary world, far from the home of her childhood, far from the ones who loved her best.

Sallie gone? Sallie far away in the storm and darkness? Why no, of course not. Sallie was only a little child sleeping quietly in her own little room. See, the door was ajar and a ray of light from the lamp in Sallie's room was streaming across the kitchen floor. He must go in and extinguish the light before it awakened the sleeping child. Why had Martha left the lamp burning? Surely she must know it would disturb the child. Well, as soon as he was rested he would go and put it out.

How tired, how tired he did feel! He'd worked pretty hard to-day, and the sun had been hot, so hot. Well, never mind, the hay was all cut now, a few more days like this and his barn would be filled with the finest hay in the country. A few more years like this one and he would be the richest farmer hereabouts. For himself, he did not care, and Martha had simple tastes like his own. But there was Sallie. She was only a wee tot now but she would be a woman some day. They must give Sallie all the advantages they had missed; they must lay by money against the time when Sallie would be a grown up woman and want things like other girls of her age.

What ailed him, anyway, that a day's work in the hay field should make him feel like this, so tired, so very tired?

He felt a little better now; he would rest a few moments more, then be off home to supper and to Martha and Sallie. But who was that calling to him? Why, Martha, to be sure, standing there by the five-barred gate. She had come to meet him with their baby in her arms. That was strange; it was not Sallie, it was their first-born, the boy with his mother's eyes who had blessed their home for only a few short months and then been laid to rest in the churchyard on the hill. The other little tots were with her, three of them, clinging closely to her skirts. They were all smiling and holding out their hands to him in invitation. But Sallie, where was Sallie? Once more Martha called his name. At the sound of her voice all the wonder, all the worriment, fled from Tony's heart.

"Coming, Mother, coming," he called happily, and the smile upon Martha's face was reflected on his own.

Christmas morning dawned bright and clear; the storm had passed in the night. Something else had passed, too - the soul of an aged farmer. It was not until the next day they found him, still sitting in the lounging chair by the stove in which only a small heap of charred ashes remained. They looked upon that serenely smiling face, then from one to another, and sadly shook their heads. One of their number stepped forward and with trembling fingers placed in the stiff, cold hand of old Tony, the letter for which he had watched through long and weary years, the letter that had come too late.

Too late? Nay, not so. Those standing by could not see, as Tony saw, the woman who lay dying in the great hospital down in the city. They could not see, as Tony saw, the last rites of the Church administered, the Sisters of Charity bending near praying, praying for that soul about to depart upon its last long journey. They could not hear, as Tony heard, the pale lips speaking their final words:

"You wrote the letter, Sister?"

"I wrote the letter, dear. It must have reached them by now."

"You told them I was dying? You asked them to forgive?"

"I told them all and I'm sure they have forgiven already."

"Dear father and mother! God bless them both! God have mercy upon me!"

They could not know, but Tony knew. Perhaps that explained the smile on Tony's face, the smile they could not comprehend.

Isabel Cecilia Williams

THE TRAMP

"A pretty tough looking character, that! But I suppose you see a great many just such specimens in this quaint little town of yours."

Father Antony's back was turned to the speaker and for several moments he remained standing at the top of the veranda steps, following with his eyes the slouching figure that had just passed through the gate and was tramping slowly along the county road. Then, with a sigh he returned to his seat and, running his fingers through his hair, remarked half absently:

"Poor fellow, he looked almost exhausted. I tried to persuade him to remain here a little longer and rest for a spell. What a life theirs is! Some of them, of course, really enjoy it, but others -. Ah, me! Those poor others. And somehow that tramp who has just left us seems to me to belong to the latter class rather than to the former. But pardon me, Father, what was it you were just saying? I was so interested in my tramp that I failed to catch your words."

"I merely remarked," returned the younger priest, smiling, "that you must see a great many of these nomadic individuals in this quaint little town of yours. I have been here but a week and that is the sixth villainous looking rascal who has presented himself and demanded something to eat."

"Yes, a large number of tramps pass through here in the course of a year, for we are on the direct road between the two largest cities of the State. Many of them are, as you say, villainous looking, but I do not think they are half as bad as they look. In fact, in some cases, I have found them to be pretty good fellows once you had passed the rough exterior and reached the real man underneath."

"You must have had some very interesting experiences with these tramps of yours; have you not, Father?" asked the younger man curiously. "I wish you would tell me some of them."

Father Anthony shifted his chair so as to command a better view of the road. He watched in meditative silence until the tramp had become a mere blot upon the whiteness of the dusty road and had finally disappeared over the brow of a distant hill. Then he spoke in tones of reminiscence:

"It was on just such a May evening as this, clear and beautiful only much cooler, that I sat in this very chair and watched the road as I am doing now. But on that evening I watched anxiously, divided between hopes and fears, for the figure that was so long in coming; I was watching for Jim, the tramp. Jim had promised faithfully, but with some men promises are made only to be broken. I began to fear that Jim was one of these. Still I prayed fervently and continued to hope, though the twilight deepened and brought no sign of my vagrant.

"My meeting with Jim had come about in this way. For some time I had been playing a game of hide and seek with a certain backsliding member of my congregation. The hiding was all on his side, the seeking on mine. Try as I would I could not seem to obtain an interview with him. He was never at home when I called; so I decided that my only chance of coming to close quarters with the enemy was to surprise him at his work. That afternoon I had gone to the quarries and found my man superintending the gang in charge of the stone-crusher. He certainly was surprised and not very pleased to see me, and all I could obtain from him after more than an hour of argument and pleading was a promise that 'he would think about it.' The 'it' referred to the making of his Easter duty, the time for which had nearly expired. Bitterly disappointed, and with a feeling of utter defeat, I was turning away when my steps were arrested by a not unpleasant voice:

"'Why don't you try your hand on me, Father? I'm a black enough sheep to keep you busy for a few moments anyway.'

"I wheeled around and found myself confronted by a short, thick-set man of most unattractive appearance, a man whom you would scarce choose as a companion along a lonely road at night. At a glance I sized up my new acquaintance: a typical tramp who had taken a job at stoking the engine to vary the monotony of the road. He was no professional 'hobo,' but belonged to that class who take to tramping from necessity rather than from choice - a too great love for the bottle being the necessity. They find an odd job here and there, hold it until pay day, squander the month's earnings in the nearest saloon, then on again in search of a job somewhere else.

"I am well acquainted with these men, but there was something about the rough looking specimen before me, a certain something in his manner, in his speech, in the twinkle of his eyes, which set him apart from the rest of his class. A grizzled beard of iron grey concealed the lower half of his face, and the right temple and cheek were disfigured by a scar which gave the countenance a decidedly sinister appearance. In spite of that I felt that the man before me had at one time been accustomed to a very different life from the one he was leading now.

"'Why don't you try your hand on me, Father?' he repeated, and the smile accompanying the words made the ugly face almost pleasing.

"There was not time for a lengthy conversation, the engine requiring constant attention, but the tramp volunteered the information that he answered to the name of Jim, and promised to report at the rectory in the evening and give me a chance to try my hand on him.

"In the evening, then, I sat and waited, half fearing that he had changed his mind and would not come. But just as the first pale stars began to twinkle in the sky Jim pushed open the gate and I went to meet him with both hands extended in warmest welcome. He gave me his left hand, and for the first time I noticed that the right was gone - amputated at the wrist. Jim saw my glance of shocked pity and smiled as he said calmly:

"'It was the drink did it, Father - the hand and this scar on my face. I'd been hitting it up pretty lively and didn't realize where I was walking. The track wasn't wide enough for me and the train. One of us had to get off, and as the engine was the stronger of the two - well, you see the result before you.'

"'How long have you been tramping, Jim?' I asked.

"'More years than I care to think of now, Father. The drink again. In fact, it's been the drink at every turn; it's ruined my life, made a complete fool of me. But let's get down to business; only, you'll have to help me out, it's so long since I went to confession I've almost forgotten how.'

"'Come into the house or the confessional in the church,' I suggested.

"'The house or the confessional in the church? No, thank you, Father. My little friends up yonder, those pretty, sparkling stars, my only companions on many a lonely night, have been the witnesses of my degradation. Let them now behold my restoration to the favor of the God whom I've offended.'

"Strange words, those, from a tramp, and I marveled at them. Without more ado we 'got down to business,' and it was nearly two hours later when we parted at the gate. In answer to a question of mine, Jim replied whimsically:

"'Where do I live while I'm working on this job? Well, you see,

Father, I am rather particular with regard to my lodgings, and as there is nothing around here that quite suits me, I just crawl under the engine and sleep there.'

"'But when it rains, Jim?'

"'Well, it just rains, that's all.'

"The next morning Jim attended my Mass and received Holy Communion, and every morning after that when I entered the church to offer up the Holy Sacrifice the first person I would see would be my one-armed tramp kneeling in a far corner, his rosary slipping through his fingers. The rosary had belonged to his mother, and during all his years of tramping he had guarded it as his most precious treasure. He had worn it in a little chamois bag suspended from a string around his neck, but had not used it in many, many years. He came regularly one evening in each week to make his confession and to have a little chat with me. As the summer progressed I wondered more and more at this strange new acquaintance of mine; this rough looking tramp with the manners of a gentleman and the speech, except for a few lapses in the vernacular of the road, of a man of considerable education. The oddest thing of all was the feeling I had that somewhere, at some time, Jim and I had met before. Little tricks of voice and expression would seem strangely familiar.

"The summer gradually faded into autumn, and one evening in late September when I stood at the gate to say good-night to my tramp, he remarked sadly:

"'This is good-by as well as good-night, Father. I have given up my work here and am off early in the morning.'

"'Not the road again!' I cried, and the next second would have given anything to recall the thoughtless words. A pained look crossed Jim's face, but he answered quietly:

"'No, Father, not the road. Never again shall I return to that life. I have saved my wages this summer and am going back into the world to begin life all over again. This time, with God's help, I shall not make such a muddle of it as I did before.'

"The next day he was gone, and many a night as I sat over my study-fire reading or trying to work up my sermon for Sunday, my thoughts would stray from the subject in hand and wander out into the world in search of my friend the tramp. I would listen to the wintry blasts whistling down my chimney and wonder where Jim was, and wonder still more at his complete silence. Surely he might let me know if all were well with him. Had he persevered? Or had he, perhaps, lapsed into his former ways, and was he, even now, tramping the highways and byways?

"Winter passed and spring came; still no news of Jim. Another summer, another fall, another winter. Silence, absolute silence on the part of my tramp. Then, one evening in May, exactly two years from the day when I first met him, Jim stood before me once again. I recognized him by the missing right hand and the scar on the temple. Aside from those two points and the old merry twinkle in his eye he bore absolutely no resemblance to my tramp of two years ago. The face was smooth shaven, the bloat, caused by years of drinking, had all disappeared, and he looked at least ten years younger than my former friend. His ragged tramp's garb had been replaced by neat garments such as a fairly prosperous business man might wear. His whole appearance seemed to indicate that Jim had done well in the world to which he had returned. Sitting in the garden, he told me all about it.

"Yes, he had done well. It had been hard at first, oh! very hard. There had been a time when, his savings all gone and no employment in sight, he had faced actual starvation. But the darkest hour comes before dawn, and that had been Jim's darkest hour. From then on things began to mend. He had obtained a good situation and was happy in it. He had not written because for long, for so very long, he had no news but bad news to send. There was nothing but ill-luck and misfortune to report, and he waited from day to day hoping things would brighten. Then, when the unexpected stroke of good luck came, he decided to wait yet a little longer until he could bring me the good news in person.

"All the time he was talking I watched his face carefully. That puzzling, baffling resemblance to some one whom I had known was stronger than ever since the beard which concealed so much of his face had been removed. I became more and more convinced that we had met before, but when and where? I racked my memory, but the name, the personality I wanted, eluded my grasp. Something of my thoughts must have shown in my face, for when Jim finished his narrative he threw back his head, laughing merrily at my very evident perplexity.

"'It is really too bad to keep you guessing any longer, Father,' he said. 'Let me help you to remember when and where we met before. Listen and I will tell you a little story.

"'It is Commencement day at a certain large college in a certain city which we need not name. The graduating class have met together for the last time in their own particular class-room. The saintly, white-haired priest who has watched their progress step by step from the day they first entered college stands before them. He speaks words to them which brings tears to those young eyes, accustomed, as a rule, to looking only on the merry side of life. He speaks words of true affection, of gentle admonition and fatherly advice. He gives to each youth a tiny silver medal of our Blessed Mother, and exacts from each one a promise that he will faithfully carry that little medal until the day of his death.'

"As Jim spoke he took from an inner pocket a small medal of our Lady and laid it on the palm of his hand. I drew forth my rosary, and there, beside the crucifix, hung a medal the counterpart of Jim's. He smiled as he continued:

"'I see you remember now, Father, but listen just a little longer for my story is not finished. From that class-room those lads went forth into the busy world of men and of affairs. They went their separate ways, each one to fill that position in life to which he felt himself called, most of them fired by ambition and confident of success.

"'One of those young men left the college that night with his heart as buoyant and hopeful as any of his companions. Almost from the first, however, things seemed to go wrong with him. He was an orphan, father and mother having died a few years before. Perhaps if either parent had been at hand to warn him of the dangers into which he was drifting, his life might have been different. Perhaps, even if some one had warned him, the warning would have passed unheeded. He tried law for a time and did not like it; tried business and gave that up; drifted from one thing to another, always drifting lower, lower, until at last he found himself an outcast and a wanderer. For some years he lived the life of a vagrant. If at times a longing to return to better ways, a longing for all that might have been, stirred faintly within him, the feeling was quickly drowned by recourse to the one thing to which he remained faithful, the enemy that had brought about his ruin, drink.

"'During his wanderings he picked up odd jobs here and there, and one day he is taken on by the boss of the stone-crusher over there in those quarries of yours. They were badly in need of some one to stoke the engine, and even a rough looking tramp was welcome. That same day there comes to the place a certain priest who is searching for one of the stray sheep from his own fold. The tramp recognizes the priest at once, and the sight of that familiar face brings back the old, happy days of his innocent boyhood. The priest commences to speak; he pleads, he reasons with the boss of the stone-crusher. In spirit the tramp is once more back in the college chapel listening to the saintly old man who had been his guide and confidant in youth, and who had long since passed to his reward. The vague, discontented longing for better things rises up in full strength. After all, why not? The look on the priest's face as he turns away decides him. That look of bitter disappointment, of real grief, on the face of his old college friend is more than the tramp can stand. He speaks, the priest turns to him, and - well, the rest of the story you know for yourself, Father. That is, the rest as far as any mortal can relate it. The end is not yet, but I trust that end will be one which will satisfy even you.'"

Silence reigned for several moments, the fragrant silence of a warm May night. And then:

"I am sure it will, I am sure it will," mused Father Anthony, smiling confidently. "I have no fear as to what the end will be for Jim, my one-armed tramp."

"But the other man, Father, the boss of the stone-crusher? What has become of him?"

"Oh! that little game of hide and seek is still going on, but I have not lost hope even yet. God's mills grind slowly and we must abide His own good time, His own good time."

"HE HATH PUT DOWN THE MIGHTY."

"*Magnificat anima mea Dominum.*" The exquisite voice rose and fell daintily on the incense-laden air.

"*Et exultavit spiritus meus in Deo salutari meo,*" responded the chorus in triumphant harmony.

It was a Sunday evening in early June and the hour for Vesper service at Saint Zita's convent. Reverend Mother mounted the staircase leading to the chapel, then paused, with her hand upon the door, to listen as the wonderful soprano again took up the refrain:

"*Quia respexit humilitatem ancillae suae.*"

"Poor child, poor child," whispered Reverend Mother, opening the door and gliding noiselessly to her stall, where she knelt with bowed head and prayed as she had never prayed before; prayed in fear and trembling for the future of the girl whose voice had earned for her the title of "the nightingale of Saint Zita's."

Reverend Mother had always dreaded the day when she must part with this dearly loved child who had been entrusted to her care some ten years before. A gentleman had come to Saint Zita's bringing with him his little daughter of six. A man of grave, even stern aspect, there was yet a look in his eyes which filled the nun's heart with a great pity; it was the look of one who had suffered deeply and in silence. He was a man of few words and his errand was quickly explained. He was obliged to be absent from home the greater part of the time and could not attend to the education of his little girl as he would like to do. His wife was not of our faith and was also too busily occupied to look after the child. He did not mention that her occupation was that of society butterfly, who sacrificed homelife, husband and child in the pursuit of pleasure. Would Reverend Mother kindly undertake the charge of his little Nita's education, spiritual as well as intellectual? Would she be to the child what father and mother ought to be and could not?

Reverend Mother had gladly undertaken the task, and since then Nita had never been separated from her even for a day. During the vacations, when other pupils scattered far and wide to their various homes, Nita had remained at the convent, roaming at will through the deserted class-room and beautiful grounds. She was the pet and darling of the entire community. In the long summer afternoons when the nuns carried their sewing out to the orchard behind the house, or to the pine grove on the hill, where one could obtain such a lovely view of the river, Nita would flit about amongst them like a veritable woodland fairy. Her snatches of song and merry laughter made sylvan echoes ring and brought smiles to the faces of the simple women who watched her with loving sympathetic glances.

Many a time, especially of late, had Reverend Mother looked at her with anxious foreboding in her eyes. What would the future hold for this child of hers, endowed as she was with singular beauty and a wonderful voice? She was a docile child, sunny and sweet-tempered, and that very pliancy of nature was what caused the nun many a moment of uneasiness. What would become of her once she had left the shelter of her convent home and was exposed to the influence of the light-hearted, merry, soulless mother from whom she had inherited her beauty; the mother whose only god was pleasure, whose one ambition was to be the best dressed, the most popular, the most envied woman in her set. The only hope lay in keeping Nita at the convent as long as possible, or at least until her character had developed sufficiently to enable her to enter her mother's world and hold her own against it. Still, Reverend Mother dreaded the day when she must part with her child, and now that the parting had come so unexpectedly, so much sooner than she had anticipated, it was doubly hard to bear.

The nun knelt in the chapel that June evening and prayed with all her heart, not only for the future of the girl whose voice filled the air with such exquisite melody, but also for help to break to that girl as gently as possible the sad news awaiting her. Word had just arrived that her father lay dangerously ill and Nita must hasten to his bedside if she wished to see him once more in this world. The carriage was waiting and Nita must go at once.

The Benediction over and the lights extinguished, all save the tiny radiance of the Sanctuary lamp, with a final appealing glance towards the Tabernacle door, Reverend Mother left the chapel, descended to her office, where she was accustomed to interview the pupils each in turn, and summoned Nita to her presence.

A little later she stood at the foot of the convent steps and watched the carriage drive away with a weeping, forlorn little figure huddled in one corner, while the good lay-sister who accomanied her vainly essayed words of cheer and consolation. She watched with tear-dimmed eyes as the carriage rolled rapidly down the avenue and out through the gate, then entered the house and repaired at once to her refuge in all trials and afflictions that might beset her way, the convent chapel. There, with her eyes on the little golden door behind which the dearest and best of Comforters is always waiting for the sorrowful, the sin-laden, the weary-hearted, to come to Him, she found consolation and peace. Her child was in the Lord's hands and surely in those hands she would be safe.

Many times have the June roses blossomed and fallen since the night on which Reverend Mother stood in the convent doorway and watched the departure of the carriage which was bearing her child away from her out into the world of suffering and sin. Once more, the June sunshine is flooding the land and the air is heavy with the odor of June blossoms. In a small town in the south of France, a young woman, gowned in deepest mourning, sits by her own casement and gazes gloomily, despairingly, out into the gathering twilight. On a table at her side is a small pile of money which she has counted over and over again in the vain hope that she may have made a mistake and that, perhaps, after all, the amount is not quite so small as she has made it out to be. That little pile of money represents her entire worldly wealth, and when it is gone what is to become of her? Work? She glances at the soft, delicate hands resting idly in her lap. Their whiteness is dazzling as compared with the black of her gown, and she smiles rather bitterly. What work could hands like those perform? They are beautiful certainly, but useless, absolutely useless, just as she herself is useless. There is not one thing by which she can earn her daily bread, and earn it she must or starve. To what a pass has she come; she, who at one time had wealth at her command and the world at her feet.

As she sits there, broken in spirit, broken in health, a middle-aged woman in appearance, while in years not much beyond her first youth, she recalls those triumphs of her past. Her success had been marvelous though short-lived. Her mind wanders back to the days when she was the pet and idol of musical Europe. The mere announcement that she was to sing would pack the largest opera house to the very doors. Ah! Those days of triumph, when she had passed from one success to another, when the mighty ones of the earth were pleased to do her honor, when the incense of praise and flattery was burned day and night upon the shrine of her greatness. Her mother was with her then, the beautiful, fairylike little mother for whom her love had been almost worship. Her voice had been with her, too, that voice at which two continents had marveled. Both are gone now, the beautiful mother, the wonderful voice; gone, gone forever, and she is alone in the world, alone and poor and friendless.

She recalls the first and only time when she appeared in public in America, her native land. She did not want to sing that night, for her mother, who had been slightly ailing for some time, seemed very much worse. She had decided not to appear at all, but had finally yielded to the mother's entreaties and driven to the opera house. What an ovation she had received that night! She could see it all again: the lights, the flowers, the music, the vast audience simply frantic with delight at her performance. At the close she had been recalled again and again, and those enthusiastic plaudits still rang in her ears. How little she had dreamed as she smiled and bowed her thanks, and how little those who watched her had dreamed that never again was that wonderful voice to be heard by mortal ears, that voice which had stirred millions of hearts and made its owner one of the foremost singers of her day.

She had driven home from that scene of triumph to find that her mother's condition had become alarmingly worse in the few hours of her absence, and before morning she had stood beside a deathbed the recollection of which makes her shudder even now. The poor, pretty butterfly, her short summer over, fought frantically but vainly against the annihilation which was coming upon her. The memory of her early training at Saint Zita's, the memory too of that other death-scene she had witnessed when her father had passed away so calmly, so peacefully, with his eyes upon the crucifix and the words of God's minister ringing in his ears, came to the girl and she had begged to be allowed to send for a priest. Her mother had never professed any belief, but it seemed terrible to Nita to have her die without even a prayer to help her in that last awful moment. Entreaties were of no avail. The idea of a priest, of religion, of even a final prayer, was laughed to scorn. Besides, she was not dying. She was young yet and was going to have many more years of sunshine and pleasure before sinking into the oblivion of the cold, dark grave. No, no, let them not speak of death, that fearsome, awful spectre. She was going to live. Take it away, take it away, that dreadful thing standing there beside her, laying its icy hand upon her forehead. Its touch was turning her to stone. She was cold, and it was growing so dark she could see nothing. Why did they not bring lights; why did they not take away the dreadful thing beside her bed?

The final struggle was fearful to behold, and even now Nita is haunted day and night by the scene. Even now, there are times when she springs from her sleep with a cry of terror, thinking she is again assisting at the departure of that poor soul who fought so frantically against the power of death.

With her mother, a large part of their income died also, but she still had sufficient money to supply her wants. Her voice, too, was a fortune in itself; managers all over the country were eager and anxious to sign a contract on any terms she chose to dictate. The shock of her mother's death so unnerved her that she decided to spend a year in rest and travel before returning to the stage. She had come abroad again, but had scarcely reached London when she was attacked by a severe throat trouble. The most eminent physicians were consulted, various treatments tried, but the disease would not yield. The south of France was recommended, and hither she had come in a last vain effort to save the voice which had charmed all Europe. At first she was incredulous. Then, she hoped against hope that time would prove them wrong and that the lost voice would return some day even better and richer than it was before. Now, all her hopes are gone, all her delusions swept away. She knows she will never sing again, and here in her hand she holds the cable message which forms the last in this series of dire misfortunes which have come upon her within the last two years. It is the message which tells her that her investments have failed and that she is penniless.

She sits by her window in the June twilight, the numbness of despair taking possession of her. On the table lies all the money she owns in the world. It is sufficient to cover the few bills she owes, the salary of the woman who has traveled with her as maid and companion, and pay her passage back to her native land. But what then? America once reached, where can she go, to whom can she turn? The distant relatives, the friends who crowded around her in her days of success, anxiously seeking a smile, a word, a token of her favor, how will they receive her if she goes to them a pauper, a dependent upon their charity? There is no one to whom she can turn, no place to which she can go, and as the twilight deepens a heavier blackness settles upon the soul of the girl.

Presently the sound of music breaks in on the evening stillness, the sound of an organ responding to the touch of skilled fingers and blended with it the tones of women's voices. The nuns in a neighboring convent are chanting the evening office. The sound recalls the chapel at Saint Zita's, the orchard, the nuns, dear kind Reverend Mother. What peaceful, happy hours those were? Has she ever known real happiness since she quitted the quiet convent home of her childhood? Even in the days of her greatest triumphs, was there not always something she could not attain, the little bit more which was always wanting? But at Saint Zita's, how different, oh! how different! Happiness such as the world could not dream of ruled within its walls. She wonders what they are doing now, the dear nuns and Reverend Mother. They, too, are probably in the chapel reciting the office; some of them thinking of her perhaps. What would they say if they knew how false she has proven to all their teachings, how careless she has grown in the practice of that religion which is dearer to them than life itself?

A sentence in the last letter she received from Reverend Mother comes now to her mind. The letter reached her years before and has never been answered. The words are these:

"Dear child, you are successful and happy now, with the world at your feet, but if the day ever comes when all these things fall away from you and you stand in need of a true friend or of any assistance we can render, remember Saint Zita's is still your home and your old mother's heart is sick with longing for a sight of her child. Worldly joys must vanish, worldly hopes decay, but Saint Zita's and Reverend Mother will be here waiting for you."

How she longs for the peace and quiet of the old home and the comforting touch of Reverend Mother's kind arms about her! What is it that the nuns are singing! The "Magnificat." She listens in silence for a few moments, then, a strange smile curving her lips, she recites in unison with the choir:

"*Deposuit potentes de sede.* Yea, Lord, Thou hast indeed put down the mighty."

It is not until after the voices are stilled, long after the world is wrapped in slumber, that the girl turns from her open window and gathers together the small store of money on the table beside her, repeating to herself the while, slowly, half absently:

"I wonder; I wonder."

* * * * *

Another year has rolled around and again the June roses in the garden at Saint Zita's fill the summer air with their heavy fragrance. The convent door opens and Reverend Mother steps out into the portico accompanied by a caller, one of the "old girls" come back to pay a fleeting visit to the home of her childhood. The nun has changed but little with the passing of the years, but those who love her best note with anxious eyes the slight stoop of the shoulders and feebleness of gait.

The visitor glances idly at a lay-sister who is busily engaged sweeping the long flight of stone steps leading from the portico to the driveway below. Her glance passes over the insignificant figure of the lay-sister, and, looking across to the pine grove on the hill, she speaks to Reverend Mother.

"Do you know, Mother, every time I stand here and look at those trees I am reminded of Nita, 'the nightingale of Saint Zita's,' as we used to call her. That grove was ever her favorite resort and even the odor of pines makes me think of her. I wish I knew what had become of her. I witnessed her performance the only time she sang here in America, and truly, it was wonderful. Then she disappeared completely from the face of the earth, as completely as if the ground had opened and swallowed her. Rumors came of her travels in England and the south of France and after that no news of her could be obtained. Occasionally, my dear Mother," and the visitor smiled knowingly; "occasionally I have fancied that you knew her whereabouts and could tell us of her."

"You are right, dear child, I could tell you, but I may not."

"At least, Mother, tell me this: She is well and happy?"

"She is well, indeed, and I think I may safely say happier than she has ever been before."

"Thank you, Mother," and the visitor descends the steps and is gone.

"Sister Gabrielle," calls Reverend Mother gently.

The lay-sister approaches, her broom still in her hand.

"You heard our conversation, Sister?"

"Yes, my Mother."

"I spoke truly, did I not, dearest child?" and the old eyes peer anxiously into the depths of the younger and smiling eyes raised to meet her gaze.

"You spoke truly, my Mother. Never before have I known what real peace and real happiness were. Never, did I dream that life on earth could be as mine is, so happy that it seems to me a little foretaste of the joy the angels must know in heaven. *Deposuit potentes de sede, et exaltavit humiles.*"

A MEMORABLE CHRISTMAS MORNING

On the outskirts of one of our large mill towns, at the very end of a narrow street lined on each side by a row of dwelling houses of the poorer class, stood a tiny cottage. It was a humble, unpretentious abode of only four rooms, but it was home to the weary girl struggling up the hillside. The tired eyes brightened and lagging steps quickened involuntarily as she turned the corner and saw the welcoming light streaming from the kitchen window.

It was very late on the eve of Christmas day and the street was deserted save for the solitary figure hastening towards that beacon light of home. Darkness and silence reigned in most of the houses she passed, and she sighed as she said to herself:

"Poor mother! Still up and still at work. I wish she would not work so hard; there is no need for it now."

Reaching the kitchen window, she stood for a moment to take note of the little scene within. By the table her mother sat sewing, her head bent over her work and fingers flying as she plied the needle in and out. As the girl watched, the mother looked up at the clock on the shelf above the stove, shook her head sadly, and hastily brushing away the tears which spring to her eyes, resumed her sewing.

"Poor mother!" again sighed the girl. "Worrying about Tim, as usual, I suppose." Then opening the kitchen door, she stepped into the welcome warmth and light of home.

"Well, little mother," she cried cheerily; "here I am at last, and I suppose you thought I was never coming. You see, dear, we had to work very late to-night to finish a large order. Then there was confession and I was delayed there quite a while. I was almost the last to be heard and it was considerably after ten by the time I left the church. Everyone in town seemed to be going to confession to-night."

"Not everyone," said her mother sadly. "There is *one* who has not been in spite of his promise to us and to the Father."

The girl glanced quickly at the table on which plates for two were laid, then at the supper keeping hot upon the stove, and exclaimed rather bitterly:

"So Tim is away again, as usual, is he? And he promised faithfully to come home early to-night and go to confession for Christmas. But then, he promised the same last Easter and every First Friday since, and has broken his word every time. Mother, how long is it now since Tim has been to Mass or to confession?"

"I do not like to think, child; it's a pretty long time. I can't understand what has come over him. He used to be such a good boy, such a help and comfort to me, and now he is slowly breaking my heart. I've had trials enough, trials enough, as you know, but I never complained. I never murmured till now. I was always ready to say: 'God's will be done.' But this, this is different. Long ago, when you and Tim were children, and the twins upstairs were but a few weeks old, and your father met with that accident that crippled him for life, I only said: 'God's will be done.' All through the years he lingered in sickness and suffering and I had to work day and night, day and night to support you all, I still said only: 'God's will be done.' All through that long, hard fight to keep starvation from the door, when I saw my little children crying at times with cold and hunger, and watched my husband slowly dying and was unable to give him any of those little comforts and luxuries which the sick require, my only words were: 'His holy will be done.' But in this, the worst of all the trials that have come to me, when I see my boy drifting away from us all, turning his back on God and his religion and wandering away night after night with careless, jovial companions, intent only on the pursuits of pleasure and folly; God help me, I simply cannot bow my head and say: 'God's will be done'"; and tears streamed unheeded from the mother's eyes.

The girl stepped quickly to her mother's side and drew the gray head gently to her shoulder, whispering comfortingly: "There, there, little mother, don't cry so. You are fretting yourself to death over Tim, and surely, surely, things will come right in the end. Tim is not a bad boy, mother dear, only a little wild just now. Remember how good he used to be, how kind, how helpful, in that hard time you were just speaking about. Remember how good he was when father died, and how young he was when he first went to work to help you support us all. Tim's a good boy at heart, mother, and he's bound to come back before long."

"Yes, dearie, that's what the Father says," returned her mother, slowly drying her eyes and rising to lay the girl's supper upon the table.

"He says not to worry but just pray, pray, pray, and Tim will surely come back before long. But there, dear, sit down and eat your supper; then we'll fill the children's stockings for I can guess what is in all those parcels you brought home. Poor little things, it would not be Christmas for them unless they hung their stockings. Thank God, I've always managed to find something to put into them if it was only an orange or an apple and a little candy. Indeed, that's about all it was when you and Tim were younger, but life is so much easier now that you are helping me."

"And it is going to be easier still, mother dear, and you will be the happiest little woman in the world one of these days. This wild spell of Tim's is bound to pass and then he will settle down and be his own old self again. There, dear," the girl continued, a few moments later; "my supper is finished and now I'll clear away these dishes and fill the children's stockings. Just see all the pretty things I've brought for them. Won't their little eyes dance when they see them! Then, mother dear, before we go to sleep, you and I will say the rosary for Tim. It is too late for him to go to confession to-night, but wherever he is, and God alone knows where he may be, he needs our prayers and he will have them. As the good Father said, we will pray, pray, pray. If we only pray hard enough and trust hard enough, things are bound to come right in the end."

The afternoon and evening had been unusually busy ones for Father Xavier. Hour after hour he had sat in the confessional listening to the tales of sin and sorrow that were poured into his ears. Hour after hour he had spent bestowing the priestly absolution on the repentant sinner, giving fatherly advice and consolation to the sorrowful, sending all those troubled souls away lighter and happier for his ministrations. Hour after hour he had waited, hoping against hope, for the sound of the one voice above all others which he most desired to hear.

In a town like that which formed Father Xavier's parish, the pastor is indeed the father of his flock. Every man, woman and child is known to him personally, and he takes a direct interest in each one's welfare. As Father Xavier sat that Christmas eve and listened to the confessions of his people, his heart grew sad and hope gradually died away as he waited in vain for the voice of one whom he was striving to bring back to God and to his duty.

The crowd of penitents melted away one by one, the few last stragglers had been heard, and still the priest waited in his confessional. The boy might possibly come even yet, his boy whom he had loved with a special affection ever since he was a tiny little chap first learning his prayers in the baby class of the Sunday-school. Why was it he had not been able to hold the boy? Why had he not been able to prevent his wandering away with bad companions, this absolute neglect of all religious duties on the part of his boy? Why could he not succeed in bringing him back again even though the boy had wandered far afield?

Father Xavier had hoped much from this Christmas eve, for Tim had promised faithfully to make his confession and to start anew in the path from which his feet had strayed. Tim had promised it as his Christmas gift to the Father. Yes, Tim had promised, but Tim had broken his promise.

With a sigh of utter weariness, weariness of body, weariness of mind, Father Xavier rose and left the confessional. He glanced over the church; it was empty. He glanced towards the altar and his eyes rested on the sanctuary lamp which appeared to be burning with unwonted brightness.

The hour was late, much later than he was accustomed to keep the church open, still he lingered, unwilling to give up a last forlorn hope that his boy might yet keep his promise. With eyes fixed on the Tabernacle door, the priest knelt and commenced to recite the rosary, pleading, pleading for his boy. The joyful mysteries were finished and no one came; the sorrowful, still no one; finally, the glorious mysteries, and still the priest was alone.

With one last appeal for the welfare of that wandering soul, Father Xavier rose from his knees and walked to the door of the church to close it for the night. He passed out on the steps and stood for a moment listening to a band of roisterers that were coming up the street disturbing the peaceful quiet of the night with their noisy songs and laughter. Where was his boy at that moment? He might possibly be with this very band of half-drunken revellers who were even now passing by and would soon be swallowed up in the darkness of the street. If not with this band, he was probably wandering somewhere with another just like it. Where was his boy at that moment? The priest turned, re-entered the church, and locking the door, passed up the aisle extinguishing the lights as he went along. He stood before the altar and once more looked at the sanctuary lamp. It was certainly burning with unusual brightness to-night. It set weird, fantastic shadows dancing along the walls and peopled the dim recesses of the church with goblin shapes. It seemed beckoning to him, calling to him, drawing him gradually to the steps of the altar, where he sank upon his knees to pray once more for his wandering boy.

For yet an hour the priest lingered before the Tabernacle. Then, utterly worn out in mind and body, he passed through the sacristy, locked the door, and mounted the steps of his own house to seek a few hours of rest before commencing the arduous duties of Christmas day.

The church and rectory were situated on a hill and the priest stood in his doorway and looked down upon the town below. It was now after midnight, but many lights were still burning and the faint sound of distant merry-making reached the priest's ears. Was his boy down there among the revellers?

Beyond the town lay the river, frozen, dark and still; and beyond that again shone the lights of the neighboring city. Was his boy over there beyond that dark, silent river? Was he over there in the city in some one of those dens of iniquity which had lured so many young men to their ruin?

Well, wherever the boy was he must be left now to the care of God and his angel for Father Xavier had done all he could that night; and the priest went in and closed the door.

At that same moment, in a little cottage at the other end of the town, a sleepless mother rose from her knees beside the kitchen table and passed slowly up the stairs to her own room. The children and the eldest girl were long since asleep, but the mother could not rest for thinking of her wayward boy. Where was he to-night; where at this very moment? And he had promised, promised faithfully to turn over a new leaf with this Christmas eve. Christmas eve was here, nay, it was come and gone for midnight had sounded and it was now Christmas morning. Still, this night must be for her as all those other nights when she had lain awake hour after hour listening in silent anguish for the footstep that did not come. She had hoped much from that promise of his to Father Xavier and to her, and her disappointment was proportionately bitter.

The mother walked to the window and looked out upon the silent, frosty night. Low down upon the horizon myriads of stars were twinkling merrily, but high up in the heavens the moon shone with a brilliant radiance that totally eclipsed all lesser lights. The night was very still, very beautiful, but the silence and the beauty failed to bring peace to the mother's heart. She looked up into the heavens. How placidly cold the moon looked back at her, the same moon that was probably shedding its beams upon her boy at that moment and could tell her where he was if it could but speak. Why, oh why, could those beams not speak and tell her what they saw; why could they not bring her some message from the absent one! She had never felt like this before, she had never felt so restless, so uneasy. It was impossible to think of sleep; she would pray still longer. Perhaps the boy needed her prayers; perhaps he was in danger, danger of body, danger of soul, and needed her help. Her rosary in her fingers, she knelt by the window praying, praying, while the moonbeams danced and played around the kneeling figure. Perhaps it was just as well they could not speak and tell her what they saw out there upon the river. Perhaps they were trying to tell her and could not; trying to tell her of the three men, one of whom was scarce more than a boy, struggling out there in the icy water, struggling for life as the current sought to drag them down beneath the frozen surface. Their fingers clutched desperately at the ragged edges of the ice that had broken through with them and cracked and crumbled away at their touch.

Now but two figures were visible to the watching moonbeams; one had been dragged down into the black waters, down to his death in the freezing depths below.

For a moment a cloud covered the moon's face obscuring its view of things terrestrial. When it passed and that scene upon the river was once more visible, only one figure remained still struggling bravely; still clutching at the slippery, crackling ice; still fighting, not for life alone, but for his soul's salvation. What thoughts must have passed through his mind in those dreadful, despairing moments! Thoughts of sins committed, of graces neglected; thoughts of all that might have been and of all that was. Who can know of the sorrow and remorse that filled his heart, of the wild cry for help and pardon that went up from the river that night?

Meanwhile, the moon shone calmly, steadily, on the boy still fighting for his life, on the mother praying at her chamber window, and on good Father Xavier sleeping the sleep of the exhausted.

Somewhat later, but still before the dawn, he was summoned from that sleep to answer a sick call from the hospital just across the river, to which he was chaplain. Three young men coming home from the city shortly after midnight had attempted to cross the frozen river, though warned of the danger of doing so. The ice had broken through, two were drowned, one saved, and the doctors thought he would live though unconscious at present.

No, the names of the young men were not known as yet. The sisters at the hospital sent for the priest because the boy brought there wore a scapular and they knew he must be a Catholic. Aside from that nothing was known about him.

Father Xavier's heart stood still. Something told him that his boy had been one of those three. Two drowned, one saved! Which, oh, which was the one saved?

The hospital reached, it was with rapidly beating heart he followed the nurse through the ward and stood beside the bed at the farther end. The night light burned low and the features of the boy upon the bed were scarcely visible. Stooping low, a fervent "Thank God" broke from the priest's lips as he recognized in the silent figure, the boy for whom his heart had been yearning. His boy had been the one that was saved. Yes, saved from death, saved from worse than death, saved to carry out the resolutions he had made while struggling in the icy river that Christmas morning.

NANCY'S TALE

"Dear, dear! but God's ways are wonderful, there's no denyin' that. Many a time we poor mortals think if we only had the handlin' of things, the world would be a pleasanter place for some of us, but I reckon the Lord knows His own business best. He usually manages to bring things out right in the end, so He does."

Nancy sat before the kitchen stove, rocking to and fro, and gazing abstractedly before her. Her mood was a reminiscent one and I knew if I gave her time enough she would launch forth into one of the interesting narratives of which she possessed a goodly store. To have interrupted her train of thought by even a whisper would have been fatal; silence and patience must be my watch-words. Presently she turned to me with the query:

"'Member Mona, the old apple-woman you met here about a year ago?"

Remember the apple-woman? Indeed I did; once having met Mona it was impossible to forget her. Besides, she was, one might say, one of the landmarks of the town, the frail, shadowy little woman who sold her apples and peanuts and candy from her stand on the street-corner. Nancy's words reminded me that I had not seen Mona lately at her usual place of business.

"Well," resumed Nancy, "Mona's gone, gone forever. Poor

Isabel Cecilia Williams

Mona! It's the hard life she's had, and I'm after thinkin' she's not sorry that it's over and she's found peace an' happiness at last. Want to know her story? Well, I'll tell it to you, for it's me that can, havin' known her since we was wee scraps of babies playin' on the floor together back there in the old country. Yes, indeed, we were babies together, we grew up together, an' we come out here to America on the same ship. Dear, dear, how long ago that was, an' it don't seem much more than yesterday.

"Well, as I was sayin', times was mighty hard in Ireland that year, specially in the little town where me an' Mona was born an' reared. Crops failed, work was slack; finally, famine an' pestilence took possession of the land. Ah! child, child, you cannot dream what them words mean, famine an' pestilence. To see the rich growin' poor, the poor starvin' an' dyin' on every hand; the little children cryin' with cold an' hunger, an' the fathers an' mothers with ne'er a scrap of food to give 'em. That was the state of things in Ireland the year we left it.

"The plague had carried off my father an' mother, my brothers was all married an' moved away, an' my only sister was at service in London, so when Mona begged me to come to America with her an' Michael an' the little ones, I just jumped at the chance. Michael was a good fellow, sober an' industrious, but there was no work to be had at home and he had heard such wonders of the land across the sea. There, a man that was a man had no trouble in findin' work an' making a comfortable livin' for himself an' family. He wanted to leave Mona with his sister in Dublin, who offered to care for her an' the children until he'd made a home for 'em in the country he was goin' to. But no, Mona wouldn't hear to that. She'd promised at God's altar to take him for better or worse an' to cling to him till death. Because the worse had come, she wasn't goin' to desert him an' let him go out alone to the cold land of the stranger to fight his battle all by himself. She'd go with him an' stand by him and help an' comfort him in his struggles. She knew she could help him. She'd been taught by the nuns an' could do all sorts of fine sewin'. In America, as in

Dublin, there must be rich ladies who would pay well for a bit of fine embroidery or hand-made lace. No, no, Mona wouldn't be left behind; he must take her an' the little ones, no matter what was before them. It was settled at last that we was all to go together, an' so, one bright mornin' we stood on the deck of the ship that was carryin' us far away from home an' all we loved, far away to the strange land across the sea. With the tears runnin' down our faces, we waved farewell to the shores of Ireland, an' Mona, though she didn't know it, was wavin' farewell to happiness in this world. Poor girl, it's little she knew from that day on but grief an' trouble an' sufferin'.

"Well, child, as I was sayin', it was the fine, bright mornin' that we left Ireland, but the good weather held for only a few days after. Then, there blew up such a storm as I never see before an' hope never to see again. It was fearful, fearful. I couldn't describe it to you if I tried. We just lay in our berths, every one of us, our backs agin the wall, our knees braced agin the board in front, an' we holdin' on for dear life expectin' every moment to be dashed out on to the floor an' have all our bones broken. We was too frightened to say a word, but we prayed, oh, my! how we did pray, every mother's son of us. For nigh onto three days that poor boat struggled on bravely agin the ragin' storm, but the ship wasn't built that could live in that sea, an' the end was bound to come sooner or later. Come, it did, at last. An officer stood on the stairs orderin' us all up onto the deck; the ship had sprung a leak, the water was pourin' in faster than they could pump it out, an' we must take to the boats at once.

"I never can remember rightly what happened then. It seems now such a confusin' jumble of men, women and childer, all screamin' an' rushin' for the stairs, and all the time the wind was a howlin' an' the vessel was groanin' an' pitchin' so you had to cling to whatever was nearest to keep on your feet at all. I don't know how we got there, but the next thing I remember was standin' on the deck an' hangin' on to something to keep from bein' washed overboard by the great waves that broke over the ship an' flooded her from stem to stern. Mona stood near me with the baby on her arm an' holdin' tight to the hand of little Gerald who hid his face in her skirt an' sobbed in terror. Michael was beside her, one arm holdin' her close while with the other he hung onto the railin' just as I was doin'. Pretty soon, the boats was lowered an' everyone made a rush for 'em. There was a shout of:

"'Stand back, there, stand back! Women an' children first; only the women an' children.'

"The ship's officers an' sailors beat back the men an' commenced puttin' the women into the boats as fast as they could. One of 'em caught Mona by the arm an' tried to hurry her away. She struggled with him an' begged to be left with Michael. The sailor swore at her an' then I heard Michael's voice, calm an' steady, above the din of the storm:

"'Go at once, asthore,' say he; 'for the sake of the childer, go at once. Sure, dearie,' says he, 'we're in the Lord's hands anyway! can't ye trust Him on the water just the same as on the land?'

"The sailor lifted Mona an' the baby in his arm (it's the wee bit of a thing she was always) an' passed her on to another to be lowered into the boat. Michael caught up little Gerald an' cried out to me: 'Take the boy with you, Nancy; take him quick, girl.' But before I could lay my hand on the child I was seized and put into the boat beside Mona. The poor girl screamed and held out her arms for the little lad, but the boat was shoved off an' the last thing I can remember, as a mountain of water rolled up between us an' the ship, was seein' Michael still clingin' to the rail an' holdin' little Gerald on his arm. Then Mona fainted agin my shoulder and I had my hands full tendin' her an' the baby.

"It was nearly dusk when we took to the boat, an' pretty soon it was so dark you could scarce see your hand before you. I'll never forget the horrors of that night, indeed then I won't, tossin' on top of waves as big as mountains an' the next minute goin' down, down, down, till I thought sure we'd strike bottom before ever we come up again. But even the longest night must wear away, an' when day broke we seen a big vessel comin' towards us an' in the course of an hour or so we was all transferred to her decks. She cruised around for a time, hopin' to pick up some of the other boats, but couldn't find none of 'em. There was no tellin' how far away from the wreck an' the boats we'd drifted in the night. The vessel that picked us up was bound for America an' so we continued our voyage to this country.

"I've often heard people complain of the coldness an' hardness of the world; by 'the world,' always meanin' the folks that live in it, I suppose. To my way of thinkin' there's a deal more kindness in the world than there is selfishness an' badness, an' the people on that steamer proved me right in one case anyway. They made up a purse among 'em an' give a share to each of us that had been picked out of the sea, as you might say. So, when we landed, we each had a little money to start in with. I soon found work in a mill, an' my poor Mona managed to keep herself an' the baby by doin' fine sewin'. For a long time we kep' house together, me an' Mona, then I married an' moved away to another town. My own troubles come on me thick an' fast after that an' what with one thing an' another, an' movin' here an' there, it was years before I set eyes on her again. Then we met quite by accident an' I found she was livin' not far from here with an old woman who peddled shoestrings an' pencils on the street. Mona herself kep' a stand on a corner where she sold apples an' peanuts an' such stuff.

"That night she come to see me here an' we talked over old times an' all that had happened since last we met. She'd done well at her sewin', she said, and brought up the baby in tolerable comfort. Then, just as the child was growin' into a woman that could be of help to her mother an' pay her back for her years of workin' an' strugglin', she was took down with consumption. All the little poor Mona had managed to save went in carin' for her sick daughter an' buryin' her when she died. By that time, Mona's health was pretty well broke up, her eyes was not as good as they used to be, an' she had to give up the sewin'. She fell in with the old woman who peddled shoestrings, and, by her advice, started in with her apple-stand. They'd been together ever since an' managed to earn a livin' between 'em. We talked an' we talked that night, an' when Mona was goin' she turned to me an' says:

"'Nancy,' says she, 'I can't tell you how thankful I am to have seen you again. An' I can't tell you how much good you've done me. Nancy,' says she, 'I've been a wicked woman, a wicked, rebellious woman,' says she. 'I've said dreadful things in my heart an' felt hard an' bitter at times against Almighty God for all the trials an' sufferin' He sent me. When I look at you, I'm ashamed of myself. I've lost a husband, so have you; I lost a daughter, you lost two; my son sleeps at the bottom of the sea, but your son - .Nancy, Nancy, when I go home to-night, I'll get down on my knees an' thank God that my boy is sleepin' at the bottom of the sea instead of wanderin' the earth a shame an' a disgrace to me.'

"You see, child, that was before my Danny come back to me to be reconciled to His God. It was while he was still wanderin' I didn't know where, an' goin' from one piece of villainy to the next.

"Poor Mona, I don't believe she was half as bad as she made herself out to be, an' certainly from that day to this I've never heard a complaint or a murmur cross her lips. She's been sick, too, most all the time, an' there's been many a day when she'd ought to be home in bed but off she'd go an' stand on her corner an' peddle her apples because the old woman that lived with her was sicker than she an' they wouldn't have no money, come rent day, unless Mona went out an' earned it for 'em. Talk about the heroes that done such wonderful things that folks has to write whole books about 'em! I tell you what, child, there's many a hero hid away in the dirty little side-streets and alley-ways of every big city; only folks don't know about 'em. To my mind, Mona was one of them heroes; so sweet an' patient, pretty well on in years herself, an' all crippled with the rheumatism, but goin' out day after day to sell her apples; a slavin' an' a killin' herself for a woman a little older an' a little sicker than she was. An' all this because the old woman had been kind to her in her hour of greatest need.

"Well, after findin' her again, I seen Mona every day; she used to come here in the evenin' an' we'd sit an' talk of them that was gone. She was with me when my Danny died, an' she thanked God with me for havin' brought him back to me in the end. Then, one night, Mona didn't come, but they brought me a message sayin' she was in the hospital, dyin' rom an accident, an' wanted to see me right away. I didn't let the grass grow under my feet you may be sure, an' before long I stood beside the bed where she was lyin', her poor, pale face all drawn with sufferin'. I've called her a hero for the life she'd led, an' her end was sure enough a hero's end. That afternoon a child had started to run across the street at the corner where Mona's apple-stand was. He didn't see the horse an' team that come tearin' up the street, an' the driver was too busy lashin' the horse to see the child. In spite of her rheumatism, Mona dashed in front of the team, and with a quick shove, sent the child flyin' out of harm's away. He rolled over an' over on the street, but beyond a scratch or two wasn't hurt. But Mona fell an' the team passed over her ankles crushin' both of 'em badly. Her age an' the shock, together with her injury, made 'em sure she couldn't live long. The chaplain had been sent for, they told me, an' would come at any moment now.

"She was sleepin' when I reached her, so I sat down beside the bed an' waited. The priest come an' stood lookin' down at her, an' the kindness an' pity on his face was wonderful to see. He looked at me an' I fair jumped out of my chair with the shock his eyes sent through me.

"'Glory be to God!' I says, blessin' myself, for I was all a tremble with the fright of it. 'Sure it's Michael Conners himself come back from the dead.'

"That very minute Mona's eyes opened slowly an' fixed themselves on the priest's face. A smile that brought the tears to my eyes, it was that beautiful, crossed her face an' she held out her thin, white hand to him, whisperin', 'Michael.' Then she closed her eyes again an' was off unconscious once more.

"The priest looked first at her, then at me, an' his face was all puzzled an' amazed like.

"'How do you know that my name is Michael Conners?' says he.

"'How do you know it yourself, Father?' says I, for I had my suspicions by that time.

"'Because of this,' says he, showin' me a strangely carved little black wooden crucifix attached to his beads. 'This was on my neck when I was saved from the wreck in which my father an' mother perished.'

"'Well,' says I, 'you're wrong. 'Tain't Michael, but Gerald, is your name, an' praise be the Lord but this'll be the happy day for my poor Mona when she finds out the truth. That crucifix with the name of Michael Conners on it was given to your father on his marriage day by the priest that married him. Here's the mate to it that he give your mother on the same day,' an' I picked up Mona's rosary lyin' on the bed an' showed him the cross on it. They was as like as two peas, only on the back of hers was carved the name of Mona Conners.

"Well, we had to break the news to her gently, an' it's the happy woman she was for the next few days in spite of all the pain she suffered. She'd just lie there holdin' Gerald's hand an' gazin' at him an' makin' him tell over an' over again of how he'd been saved from the wreck. He was only a wee lad of three at the time, but he could still remember of his father standin' there on the deck of the sinkin' ship an' holdin' him in his arms. He could still hear the words his father spoke to him an' feel the father's hand slippin' the rosary over his head an' claspin' the little fingers around the cross as it lay on his breast. Michael had passed him to a sailor an' he was lowered into one of the boats, where a kind-hearted woman took compassion on his loneliness an' cared for him. They'd been picked up by a sailin' vessel bound for France, an' the woman who first cared for him, took him with her from France to America an' finally adopted him. She brought him up, educated him, an' at last he became a priest of God.

"He was with his mother to the very end, an' it was his hand that give her the last blessin' of the Church an' his voice recited the prayers that send the departin' soul safe on its journey to the throne of God. It's the happy woman my Mona was in them last few days upon earth, an' it's the happy woman she is this day, all her troubles over, all her sufferin's gone, an' she in Paradise for ever an' ever."

During Nancy's recital, the shadows of twilight had gathered and deepened, and now her little kitchen was wrapped in darkness. Still, she sat for several moments buried in thought which I cared not to interrupt. Then, with a sigh, she rose to light the lamp and I noticed that tears filled her eyes though the brave lips were smiling.

"Yes, yes," she repeated. "God's ways are wonderful, they are that. Even if we don't understand things in this world, we're sure to in the next, for the Lord knows His own business best every time."

PATSY

Patsy was wide awake in a second. What was it those men were talking about; what was it they were planning to do? That name, and "the brown house on the hill"! By a strong effort, he kept his eyes closed and breathed regularly and deeply as though still sleeping. He must not let them suspect that he was listening, but he must catch every word they said, every word. How he hated them, this band of rascals that had gotten his David into their clutches and were slowly but surely making him as bad as they! His David bad? No, no! David was kind and good and gentle to him always. David was not bad, he would not listen to their dreadful scheme. He would refuse to help them; surely he would. His David a thief? It was impossible. But that dreadful plan they were discussing! "The brown house on the hill"; "to-morrow night"; and David was promising to go with them.

Patsy shivered beneath the bedclothes and bitter tears gathered in his eyes and trickled down the pale, sunken cheeks. The men were leaving and David was renewing his promise to accompany the expedition to the brown house on the hill to-morrow night. In fact, he was to act as guide to the man appointed to commit the deed, for who, so well as David, could show them the way to the library in which was the safe that they were going to rob?

They had gone now and Patsy felt that David was standing beside the bed and looking down at him. He opened his eyes and two more tears escaped, which he hastily brushed away.

Immediately David was on his knees, the little cripple's hand clasped tenderly in his.

"What's the trouble, kid?" he questioned anxiously. "Is it the pain that's bad to-night?"

"'Tain't the pain, Davy, 'tain't the pain at all," sobbed the child.

"What is it then, youngster? Come now, tell your own Davy what's troubling you, there's a good boy."

"David, how long is it since mother was taken away from us? It seems so long. I was thinkin' of mother, Davy, and wishing she was here with us this night."

"You poor kid, poor little crippled kid," muttered David, patting the small, thin hand. "It's natural, I suppose, for you to pine for your mother, but ain't Davy been almost like a mother to you, Patsy? He's tried hard, that he has, to be father and mother and big brother all in one." And the man smiled somewhat wistfully.

"You've been all that and more too, Davy. 'Twasn't on my account I was wishin' for mother, 'twas on yours. If she was here, she'd know how to keep you from going with them men to-morrow night. She'd know how to keep you to home, and I don't know what to say or to do to stop you from going."

David's face darkened slightly and there was a note of sternness in his voice as he said:

"So you was listening, was you, and heard what we was talkin' about?"

"I didn't listen a purpose, David; at least, not at first. I happened to wake and heard 'em speak of the brown house on the hill. Then I wanted to hear everything and I listened a purpose after that. Oh, Davy! Davy!" the child cried imploringly, sitting up in the bed and clasping his hands in petition; "don't do it, Davy; don't be a thief to please those wicked men; don't go robbing the brown house on the hill."

A fearful fit of coughing racked the little form and David held him gently in his arms until the paroxysm had passed. Then, laying the boy back upon the pillows, he said quietly:

"You mustn't get excited, Patsy, it's bad for you. We'll not talk no more to-night. In the morning I'll tell you the story of the house on the hill and you'll see I'm not tacklin' this job to please anyone but myself. Go to sleep now, kid, for I'll not say another word to-night, not another word."

When David spoke in that tone of voice Patsy knew there was nothing for him to do but to obey. Turning his face to the wall, he closed his eyes, but sleep did not visit him that night. He lay listening for the stroke of the town clock as it sounded, one after another, the slowly dragging hours; he lay listening to David's regular breathing and wondered how a man could sleep so calmly with such a deed in prospect; he lay anxiously turning over in his mind various schemes by which he could frustrate the plan in case he failed in persuading David to abandon it altogether. Several times fits of coughing shook him nearly to pieces, and at those times the pain in his poor little chest was well-nigh unbearable. He smothered the cough as well as he could beneath the bedclothes for fear of disturbing David. As for the pain - well, pain and Patsy had been companions so long now that he had grown quite accustomed to it.

The next day was cold and dismal, with a leaden sky threatening snow, and a bitter wind blowing that searched the very marrow of one's bones. The few neighbors who chanced to glance out of their windows at an early hour in the afternoon were surprised to see Patsy making his way along the street, slowly and painfully, with the aid of his crutches. They had never known him to be abroad on a day like this; indeed, it was many a day since he had attempted going upon the street at all. Poor little Patsy, his crutches were once a familiar sight going up and down the pavements on pleasant days in the summer time, but they had thought never to see him leave his room again. Did David know? Some one should stop the child; he was too weak to wander out alone like that. But then, it was no affair of theirs; David could probably be trusted to look after the boy.

As no one was willing to make it his business to interfere, Patsy went on his way unmolested. A strange look of determination battled with the pain on the sickly, childish face as he made his way bravely against the biting wind that sought to drive him back. He had learned the mystery of the house on the hill; he knew now why David hated so bitterly that house and all connected with it; he knew why David was willing and eager to help the men in the plan they were to carry out that night. David had told him all about it, and for the first time in his life he had felt afraid of this dearly loved brother of his. It had been a revelation to Pasty. Surely, this bitter, unforgiving, revengeful man could not be the same who had been father, mother and big brother to the little cripple for whom he had cared so tenderly since their mother had been taken from them.

It had sounded like a fairy tale to Patsy; he could scarcely believe his own ears. Just to think of it; that brown house on the hill had once been their mother's home, and the man who lived there, the man whom David hated with undying hatred, was their mother's brother and their uncle. On the day she married, she had left her home forever, her brother vowing that never as long as he lived would he set eyes upon her face again; to him she would be as though dead. Once, when father lay dying (Patsy could not remember it, but David had told him of it), mother had written to their uncle imploring a little help in their misery. It was not for herself she had asked but for the dying husband and sickly baby. Her letter had been returned to her with these harsh words written on the back: "Some mistake here. No woman has the right to call me brother. My only sister died years ago." David had kept the letter ever since; he had been old enough at the time to understand. He had vowed then to have revenge some day and he kept the letter to remind him of the vow should he ever be in danger of forgetting it.

Patsy knew now why his brother so hated the house on the hill, and why David had been so cross on that day last summer when he, Patsy, had come home and told of the young lady who had been so kind to him, the lady who lived in the house on the hill. As a rule, every one was good to Patsy. Even the children on the street, who quarrelled among themselves, striking, reviling, pelting one another with stones, had, nothing but kind words and smiles for Patsy. But that day last summer he had wandered farther from home than usual and a crowd of rough boys had stopped and commenced tormenting him, laughing at him, calling him names, jeering at his deformity, and even pulling his hair and pinching his ears. The child had tried to push past them, but they closed in on him and it might have fared ill with Patsy but for the timely arrival on the scene of the young lady from the house on the hill.

She quickly scattered the band of hoodlums and then walked with Patsy until he was well on his way home and safe from further attack. She had been kind to him, and made him promise to come and see her. That was how he knew her name and where she lived. He had wanted to see her again and had thought of her so often but David would not let him go.

Many a night, when the pain kept him from sleeping, he would while away the long hours by thinking of the gentle, beautiful girl, and he never said his prayers at night and morning, as mother had taught him, that he did not add a petition for his "lovely lady." And to think that she was his own cousin, his uncle's daughter; she lived in the house on the hill and it was her house that David and those men were planning to rob. For her sake as well as David's the deed must be prevented; her father must not be robbed; David must not become a thief. Patsy had determined that last night when he first heard them mention the scheme. If no one else would stop them, he would, though he could not imagine how he was going to do it. He had thought and thought until his head ached so that he could hardly see, but no plan suggested itself to his mind. He prayed, too, long and earnestly, for the priest at the Sunday-school told them God would always answer little boys' prayers if what they asked for was good for them. And was it not a good thing for which he was pleading? Simply that he might find a way to keep his lady from being robbed and save David from becoming a thief?

At last, the idea he wanted had come to him; he knew just what he must do to secure his end. There was danger in the plan, to himself, but he must risk that. It mattered little what happened to him if he could only save his David, his dear, kind big brother, who would never have thought of doing wrong had it not been for those wicked men who had led him astray. Patsy feared those men mightily. He knew their anger would be terrible should they discover how their plan had been frustrated. They might even kill him if they found him out, but he hoped they need not know. He would confess to David alone at supper time that evening; no matter how angry, David would not hurt his little brother. Of that Patsy was certain. Anyway, whatever the risk, he must take it to save David and to save the lady.

The early winter twilight was closing in when Patsy reached his home again and dragged himself up the stairs to the one room which he and David occupied. He was almost exhausted and his breath came in short, sharp gasps which cut him like knives. He would have liked to crawl into his bed, close his eyes and never open them again, he was so tired. But he must not give in yet; his task was but half accomplished. David must be told of what he had done, and at that thought a spasm of fear contracted his heart. Shivering, he drew a chair near the stove and waited with closed eyes and pain-drawn face for the sound of David's foot upon the stairs.

Twilight passed and darkness filled the little room, still David did not come. Patsy lighted the lamp upon the table, wondering anxiously why his brother was so late. He put more coals upon the fire, which was burning low, and made the tea for David's supper. He set out the loaf of bread, the cold meat, the cheese, upon the table, then resumed his chair and his eager listening for footsteps that were so long in coming. It seemed to Patsy he had waited for hours and hours, and suddenly his heart stopped beating and his eyes distended in terror as a thought occurred to him. Suppose David did not come at all! What, what would happen then? But there, that was David's step and all would be well now. The child looked up eagerly as his brother entered the room, then, nearly cried aloud in his bitter disappointment. David was not alone. One of the gang was with him, and this was a contingency for which Patsy had made no allowance. What was he to do now? How could he tell his brother, how warn him, in the presence of that dreadful man?

For the first time in his life David was so preoccupied that he paid no heed to the little cripple who had now withdrawn to the darkest corner of the room and crouched there in abject terror. The two men made a hasty meal and then sat by the table talking in tones so low that Patsy heard scarcely a word of what was said. Anyway, he cared nothing for their plans now; he had spoiled everything for them. But how was he to tell David, how was he to tell David?

By and by, a third man joined them and there was more whispering with heads close together. At last, the three arose and made preparations for going out. They moved towards the door and were astonished to find themselves confronted by a small, crippled figure, that stood swaying on his crutches, directly in their way. A bright red spot burned on either cheek, the eyes were brilliant with fever, and the child was panting for breath. But he said very quietly, his eyes fixed steadily on his brother's face:

"You mustn't go out to-night, David."

The men gasped and looked at one another in amazement.

"You mustn't go out to-night, David," the child repeated. "You mustn't none of you go to the house on the hill to-night."

"We mustn't go out, mustn't we," exclaimed one of the men roughly. "Who's to stop us going, I'd like to know? Stand aside, kid, before harm comes to you."

"Who's to stop you? I am. I have stopped you."

A laugh of derision greeted this statement.

"Yes," Patsy repeated; "I've stopped you. I peached on you; I warned 'em you was comin'."

David's face was terrible to see.

"What's that you're saying, Patsy? You what?"

"I warned 'em this afternoon. I went to the house on the hill and told 'em you was comin'. You mustn't go, David, you mustn't go. The police'll be there waitin' for you, 'cos I told 'em you was comin'. I didn't want you to be a thief, David; I done it for your sake. Oh, David, David!"

David's face was livid and his clenched fist was raised to strike, but Patsy and his crutches lay in a little huddled heap at David's feet.

When the child opened his eyes again, the men were gone and he and his brother were alone. He looked into the face bending above him and gave a sigh of relief. All the anger was gone, only anxious solicitude rested there. Patsy tried to speak, but his voice was so weak and low that David had difficulty in understanding what he said. He leaned over to catch the faintly whispered words:

"You ain't mad at me now, are you, Davy? I'm so glad. I'd hate to go away thinkin' you was mad at me. I had to do it, Davy, I had to tell; there wasn't no other way to keep you from being a thief. I'm sorry to leave you alone, Davy, but I guess mother wants me in Heaven. You know the doctor said I'd be going soon anyway. Mother said she'd be waitin' for you and me and I guess she wants me now. I'm sorry to leave you, but I'm afeared I must go. It'll be lonesome for you when I'm gone. You'll have no one to light the lamp and make the tea for you in the evenings. You'll come home here at night and it'll be all dark and lonely with no Patsy to meet you. But remember, David, I'll be lookin' at you from Heaven. Mother and I'll be waitin' for you there and I'm thinkin' even Heaven won't be just right till you've come to us. Promise me you'll come to us some day; promise you'll never go with them wicked men no more. Let 'em alone or they'll make you as bad as they be, and then you won't never see mother and me. Promise you'll let 'em alone, Davy; promise you'll be good and come to us in Heaven some day."

"I promise, kid, I promise," whispered David brokenly. "With God's help I'll turn over a new leaf and I'll come to you some day."

A smile brightened the pale, pinched face, a smile of absolute content and trustful affection.

"God bless you, my Davy, God bless you," murmured the faint voice haltingly. "Good-by - until we meet - in Heaven."

THREE EVENINGS IN A LIFE

I

One by one the city clocks chimed the hour of midnight. One by one Jane counted the strokes and sighed despairingly as she glanced at the window in which the light still burned so brightly. The air was bitter cold, a fine snow was falling, and she had been trudging up and down, up and down, for ages it seemed to her. Richard was growing so heavy and her arms ached so she could scarcely hold him. Still, there was nothing for it but to tramp up and down, up and down the narrow street, the baby in her arms, until mother should give the welcome signal. When that lamp in the window opposite was put out and the house in darkness, she would know that it was safe for her to creep up the stairs and into the bed in the kitchen which she shared with the baby brother now sleeping in her arms.

Seating herself upon a doorstep she was passing, Jane shifted the baby to a more comfortable position and leaned her head against the rough woodwork of the tenement house. How tired, she was, how very tired! Her head ached, her back ached, she ached all over. Day after day, she worked in the factory from early morning until nightfall. Night after night, she walked the street with Richard in her arms, not daring to enter the house until father was safely sleeping. Of course it did not happen every night. Just once in a while father would come home sober and then there was no fear of harm to the baby or

Isabel Cecilia Williams

herself. Many a night, too, he did not come home at all, but on those occasions she and mother scarce dared to close an eye. They knew not at what moment he might return, possibly in even an uglier mood than usual. Mother was never afraid for herself. She could usually manage him, although there had been times when bad cuts and bruises bore testimony to the treatment to which she had been subjected. For Jane and little Richard, their only chance lay in keeping out of the way, so Jane would tramp the street, Richard in her arms, despite aches and pains and weariness.

The child on the doorstep anxiously watched the window across the way. Would the light never go out? Father must be unusually bad to-night, and she was so tired. The day had been a hard one at the factory and every bone in her body ached. Well, there was one comfort; to-morrow would be Sunday and she could stay at home all day. To-morrow? To-day, rather, for midnight had already passed. She would have one long day to rest and help mother. She felt now as if she could sleep the whole day through. She would like to sleep for a week at least, and even then she would not be rested quite enough. There were moments of unusual fatigue and depression in which she could almost wish that she might fall asleep and sleep forever as the other little ones had done. Three of them there were, delicate, sickly little creatures, who had struggled for a time against the ills of human existence and then given up the unequal conflict. At times, she could almost find it in her heart to envy them were it not for mother and Richard, especially Richard.

There, at last! The light was gone, the window in darkness, and it was safe for her to return to the tenement across the way.

II

The same street, the same tenement house, but grown even uglier and dingier with the passing of the years. In a small room on the second floor, Jane sits beside the bed on which her mother tosses in the delirium of fever. Her heart is slowly breaking as she listens to the moaning, insistent cry which issues from those parched lips. All through the days and nights of anxious watching, that cry has been ringing in her ears, the call for "Richard, Richard, Richard."

That her mother is dying she knows full well, and how she longs for one loving glance, for one word of affection, to carry with her in the lonely years to come. But no look of recognition comes to the sightless eyes and no word escapes the lips save that never ceasing cry of "Richard, Richard, Richard." A white-capped nurse flits softly about, but Jane pays no heed to her. The doctor enters and hold whispered consultation with the nurse. Jane does not even glance at him. She is tired of hearing him say the same old thing time after time: "While there is life, there is hope." She knows there is no hope, though everything possible has been done to save the precious life now ebbing so swiftly. Thank God, they are no longer poor as when she was a child. Her salary is a splendid one and she has been able to have the best advice, the best care possible, for her dying mother. No, they are no longer poor, but of what avail is money now? It cannot bring back the days that are gone, the happy days before Richard went away. And they were happy, then, so happy.

After her father's death, which had occurred while she was still a mere child, she and mother had devoted themselves to the task of caring for little Richard. They toiled; they starved, they saved - all for Richard. They prayed and planned and hoped - for Richard. He must go to school, he must go to college, he must become a power in the world. For themselves, poor food, poor clothes, the old tenement were good enough, for every cent they saved meant so much the more for Richard when he should have come to man's estate. And Richard? Oh! he had been well content to take all they offered him. He went to school, he went to college; only, somehow, the reports of his doings there were anything but encouraging. They seemed to be merely a series of pranks and mischief, but the devoted mother was very ready to make allowances. The boy was young, he would grow steadier as he grew older. They must have patience with him for a few years yet. At times Jane doubted the wisdom of their course, and when the demands, not only upon their patience but upon their purse, became greater and greater, Jane had counseled removing him from college and setting him to work. Not so the mother. Her cry was ever: "Patience, patience, and all will yet be well." So they bore with him a while longer to their never ceasing sorrow.

His escapades grew wilder, the reprimands of the faculty more severe. At last came the final prank, which had resulted in his disgrace and expulsion. Even then, she and mother was ready to forgive and had written him to come home. No answer from Richard had ever been received. Instead, came the news that the boy had disappeared, run away; the last seen of him was boarding a train for the West. All efforts at tracing him had proved futile, and to this day they knew not where he was.

Mother had never smiled again but had drooped and faded day by day. Time and again Jane had urged moving to more congenial surroundings, to a flat or cottage in the suburbs, to fresh air and sunshine. But no, mother would not have it so; Richard might come back some day and how could he find them if they moved away from the old home in the tenement house?

Even now, when she is dying, her last thought is not for the girl beside her, the girl who has toiled so patiently, watched so faithfully, sacrificed all so generously, for mother and for Richard. Even in delirium, her thoughts are only for the absent one; her words, that insistent, heartrending cry for "Richard, Richard, Richard." Jane bows her head in anguish but whispers low: "Thy will be done."

III

Long since, the factory whistle has sounded the signal for release from the day's toil. The workers in the factory, a small army of men and women, boys and girls, poured forth from the doorways of the huge buildings, swarmed up the street, laughing and chattering, and dispersed to their several homes. The buzz and jarring of the machinery have ceased and silence fills the place. Even the offices are deserted, with the exception of one from which issues the steady click, click, of a typewriter.

Jane Horton, private secretary and confidential clerk to the millionaire president of the company, is a very busy as well as a very important individual. The sound of that whistle means release for the workers in the rooms above, the toilers at the machines where she herself labored so many years ago; it means release for stenographers, bookkeepers, clerks, in the general office without; but for her, there yet remain many things to be attended to before she can take advantage of the half holiday and seek the seclusion of her small suburban home. Important letters must be written, private letters which cannot be entrusted to the care of an ordinary stenographer. For some time longer Jane's typewriter clicks unceasingly, and it is nearly dusk before her task is finished and she is free to lock her office door and leave the building for the night.

She walks rapidly along the darkening streets, sorry that she is so late. She fears Marie will have been watching for her all the afternoon and worrying perhaps, little Marie, the lame factory girl whom she has befriended, the girl with eyes so strangely like to Richard's. The resemblance is startling at times, though Richard's eyes were ever merry, ever dancing with fun and mischief, while Marie's are grave and sweet and sad. Still, the likeness is there, and probably that is the reason that Jane has been so anxious to help this girl, scarce more than a child, who had appealed to her for aid. Marie was by no means the first to seek her assistance in time of need, for Miss Horton's name stands for all that is kind and gracious and helpful in every department of the factory. The woman who has succeeded, who has worked her way up, step by step, to a position of trust and confidence, does not forget the time when she stood, as Marie does now, with her foot upon the lowest round of the ladder. She never forgets the days when she worked as they work, and is ever ready to extend a helping hand to those who need it. To her, then, Marie had come, as had so many others before her, in her hour of trial and distress. Hastening along the street, Jane smiles as she recalls the day Marie had first tapped upon her office door and, entering timidly, waited for permission to speak. Jane had been unusually busy and frowned impatiently at the interruption. The eyes, so like to Richard's, had quelled her anger and she listened to the girl's story.

It was Jackie was the trouble this time, Jackie who came next to her and who helped in the support of the family. He'd just broken his leg and was in the hospital and there was no telling when he would be out again. The twins were sick, too, and there were Nellie and Minnie and the little baby, and mother not strong enough to work even if she had time to leave the children. Father? Well, that's just where Miss Horton's help was needed. Father had worked here in the factory, out in the shipping-room, but they'd discharged him several weeks ago. Yes, father had been discharged before, many times before, and had been taken back again. This time they would not let him come back though he had begged and pleaded and promised faithfully never to touch the drink again. No, no, father did not get drunk very often, only once in a while, and he was never cross or ugly. He was the kindest and best of fathers only he drank a little just once in a while. Wouldn't Miss Horton please; please, say a word for father and get them to take him back? Miss Horton hesitated for a moment, looked into the eyes so like Richard's, then promised that she would.

She certainly kept her promise and said, not one word, but many, in her efforts to have Marie's father reinstated in his former position. The man was a stranger to her, she had never seen him, never even heard his name before, but for Marie's sake she pleaded his cause most earnestly. The same reply met her every turn:

"Not a better man in the place when he was sober, the very best worker we've got. But just when we're busiest and need him most, off he goes and gets drunk. Not so very often, oh! no, but always when he's needed most. We've forgiven him time again, but he's had his last chance. We'll not take him back."

Jane had even appealed to the president himself, but the appeal was useless. He never interfered in such matters, left them entirely to the department heads.

The eyes like Richard's filled with tears as Marie was told of the utter failure of all appeals. The pale face grew paler day by day and the thin figure drooped wearily. Jane had, more than once, offered pecuniary help, which had been gently but firmly refused. They'd manage somehow, Marie thought, until Jackie was well again and able to help, though it was hard to feed so many on just one girl's pay. If they would only take father back, that was all the help she needed; just for them to take father back. He'd not touched a drop now for six months and vowed he never would again. He'd taken the pledge and was making the First Fridays. He'd not missed one since he began five months ago, and oh! if they'd only give him one more chance. That's what father said himself, that's all he wanted, just one more chance to make good. He meant it this time, too, Marie was quite sure of that. If they'd only give him that one chance he'd make the most of it.

Jane Horton had promised to make one more attempt and she is now carrying to Marie the good news that her efforts have been crowned with success.

Following the directions given her, she passes from the broad, well-lighted streets to smaller, darker ones. Finally she turns down a narrow, crooked alley and enters a tumble-down house at the farther end. Bad as was the tenement home of her early

Isabel Cecilia Williams

childhood, this place is far worse, and a wave of pity fills Jane's heart as she thinks of that delicate, patient child growing up in surroundings like these. Marie herself opens the door in response to Jane's knock, her eyes anxiously asking the question her lips dare not utter.

"Good news, little one, good news," cried Jane joyously, advancing into the room and taking in at a glance the terrible poverty of the place, the shabbiness of the woman laying the table for supper, and of the barefooted, ragged children who stare at her in open-mouthed astonishment. "Where is your father, Marie? Take me to him at once for I bring him what he asked for - one more chance to make good."

In answer to Marie's call, the door leading into an adjoining room opens and a man steps forth. The light of the lamp shines full upon his face, and for one breathless moment they face each other in silence, the woman who has succeeded in life, the man who has failed, and to whom she brings one last chance of redeeming his failure.

Despite the change of name and the greater changes wrought by the hand of time, she knows him at once. It is Richard, her brother.

THE ELEVENTH HOUR

It was an ordinary tenement house of the poorest class, exactly like its neighbors, which lined both sides of the dingy street. The door was always open, more than half the time hanging by one hinge, the stairways were dark and crooked, the rooms small and dirty. In a back kitchen on the topmost floor, a man sat, or rather huddled, in a chair drawn close to the stove. His eyes were closed and his head drooped wearily against the back of the chair. That last spell of coughing had been unusually severe and had left him weak and breathless. A plague on the cough, anyway. Why was it he could not get rid of it? The doctor from the dispensary, the district nurse, even Maggie, had assured him that with the coming of summer this cold of his would be better. Summer was here, though you would not think so to-day with this raw east wind and drizzling rain, and instead of being better he was worse, decidedly worse. Could it be that they were all wrong and Nancy alone was in the right? Nancy, who, of all that approached him, was the only one who dared to tell him the truth. The truth? No, it was a lie, a lie; he was not dying, he was going to be well and strong again as soon as he could shake this cold that had settled upon him. Nancy was a meddlesome old woman. He had told her so not more than an hour ago and had sent her off about her business. He had been harsh to her and rude, and after all she was old and had probably meant to do him a kindness. But, then, he was not sorry; she'd not come bothering him any more now with her dismal croakings of death and eternity. Death? He defied it. Eternity? Time enough to think of that.

Isabel Cecilia Williams

He opened his eyes and they rested upon the chair which Nancy had occupied one hour ago, which she had occupied so frequently during the past few months. She had been almost a daily visitor since he and Maggie had been living in these wretched lodgings in "Nancy's Alley," as it was called. Evidently, the old woman seemed to think the entire street was her personal property and that she was responsible for the welfare of all the dwellers thereon. Well, he guessed he had taught her not to come meddling in his affairs. He hoped he had anyway. Dying? The idea of such a thing; how dared she tell him he was dying when everyone else fed him with the hope that he would be better to-morrow, next week, next month. Ah! yes, but to-morrow never came; or rather, when it did come, it was no longer to-morrow with its promise of renewed health. It was to-day, with the same disappointment, the same pains, the same racking cough, which he had endured on so many other to-days that had come and gone before it.

Watching the chair she had so lately occupied, he could see once more the figure of Nancy, her bright eyes and cheery smile, and hear the nimble tongue which chattered so merrily or soothed so gently according to the needs of her listener. He could see the little, stooped figure in its ragged gown, the work-worn hands, the smooth, grey hair. He would miss her visits; yes, indeed, he would miss them sorely. But what right had she to go talking to him of death? Still, she was old, she had been kind to him, and he had driven her away in anger. He had called her a meddlesome busybody who went about poking and prying into other people's affairs and had ordered her to leave the house and never enter it again.

"Pokin' an' pryin' is it?" she had answered quietly as she made her way towards the door. He remembered now how difficult it had been for her to walk even on the level floor; what a task it must have been for her to climb those three long flights of stairs as she had been doing every day for these months past. "Pokin' an' pryin' is it? Maybe so, maybe so. But Nancy didn't mean it that way, no, lad, indeed she didn't. Nancy was thinkin' of her own boy lyin' at rest out yonder with the green grass growin' over him, her own boy that went the same way you're a goin' now. He'd be about the same age as you, too, an' there's the look on your face that I seen on his so often, the desperate, despairin' look that it breaks my heart to see. I figured that if you was my boy, I'd be glad for some one to tell you the truth an' try to bring you back to God before it's too late. I'd figured, too, that most likely you had a mother somewheres. She may be still on the earth prayin' for you an' longin' for you, same as I prayed an' longed for my Danny for so many years. She may be in heaven lookin' down on us now, but wherever she is she'll be glad to know that I tried to bring you back. It's for her sake that I'm doing this, for the sake of your poor mother wherever she may be."

His mother! What memories that name conjured up! His mother who had kissed and blessed him as she closed her eyes forever so many, many years ago. He was still looking at the chair which Nancy had occupied but he saw it not. He was a boy once more standing by his mother's bedside, her soft, white hand in his, and was promising her - ah! How many promises he had made holding that dear hand for the last time, and how readily he had broken those promises every one!

His mind wandered on and he saw himself a boy at school, a youth at college, a grown man filling a position of trust in a large business concern. In those days, wherever he might turn, there was one figure standing out before all others, one friend, tried and true. When boys at school this friend had saved his life; when young men at college, it was to this friend's continued help he owed any little success he may have attained. After leaving college, his position was secured through the kindly offices of this same friend whose desk was next his own in the office in which they were employed.

His gaze still rested on the vacant chair but he saw only a pretty little suburban cottage with flower garden and smooth green lawn and box-bordered gravel paths. Once upon a time that cottage was his, and the sweet-faced girl, who trod those paths so daintily, tripping to the gate to meet him on his return in the evening, was his wife. Upstairs in the nursery their children slept, two fair little girls with their mother's pretty eyes and dainty ways. All that had been his, once upon a time.

He still watched that vacant chair but he saw only the day they discovered the loss of that money which had disappeared so mysteriously from the firm's safe. Suspicion rested upon that one true friend of his, the friend to whom he owed all he was, all he had. There was not sufficient evidence to prove that he was the thief, but in the minds of his employers there was no doubt as to his guilt. The supposed delinquent was dismissed and the cloud of suspicion rested upon him wherever he went thereafter. Only two people had known the truth, the man now sitting by the stove in the tenement house kitchen and the friend who had suffered in silence rather than betray him. They had never met again, and not long after the robbery, the man now sitting by the stove had heard of his friend's death; the physicians said it was typhoid, but he knew better. Disappointment, anxiety, heartbreak, were the real causes of his friend's early taking off.

He still gazed at the empty chair but he saw only the series of misfortunes that had befallen him since the day his friend died. He had launched into business on his own account; the result was dire disaster. His home was burned in the dead of night; they barely escaped with their lives. Everything was gone; there was no insurance and ruin and despair confronted them. His children died suddenly of a malignant fever and the heartbroken mother had followed them to the grave within a few weeks. He was alone, all alone, and from that day to this had gone steadily downward until now he found himself in this dirty tenement depending for his daily bread upon the faded, ragged little woman who was now his wife. Poor Maggie, how she irritated him at times and yet she had been a good faithful wife to him. But for her, they would not have even this miserable apology for a home. Yes, even Maggie, with her watery eyes and thin, unkempt hair, Maggie, who scrubbed floors for a living and could not write so much as her own name nor read the simplest child's primer; even Maggie was far too good for the worn-out drunkard and gambler whom she tended so faithfully.

A light tap upon the door, but the man by the stove was too much occupied with those phantoms of the past to pay heed to it. The door opened quietly and a priest stepped into the room. The man's gaze shifted from the vacant chair to the black-robed figure standing by the door and looking at him in puzzled amazement. Phantoms of the past? Yes, indeed, and here was one more come to torment him and to mock at him. The two watched each other in silence for a moment. Then, the man crouching in his chair by the fire found voice at last:

"What brings you here, you, of all men? Have you come to taunt me, to upbraid me, to delight your eyes with the sight of my misery? Have you come to laugh at me in my downfall?"

"Nay, friend," returned the priest gently, "none of those things has brought me to you to-day. I come only on a mission of mercy, to bring you peace and pardon."

"But how did you find me; who sent you to me?" demanded the man by the fire.

"A little old woman, Nancy by name, told me there was one here sadly in need of the ministrations of a priest. I did not dream that I should find *you*."

"You know me then; you remember me?"

"I remember you perfectly and recognized you at once, though you have changed almost beyond recognition."

"You say you know me, but you do not, you do not. You may know *who* I am, but you don't know *what* I am. You don't know that I'm a thief. Yes, a thief, for it was I who took that money he was accused of stealing. Do you know that?"

"I know it," answered the priest calmly, "and still I say I bring you peace and pardon."

"Perhaps you know, too, that I am a murderer, for it was grief, heartbreak, which weakened him so that when disease attacked him he had not sufficient strength to combat the fever. Do you now that, you who talk to me so easily of peace and pardon?"

"I know that, too, and it is in his name that I offer you forgiveness for your sins."

"You know all then? He told you?"

"He told me in the delirium of fever. He never knew he told; he died thinking he carried the secret with him to the grave. He was faithful even unto death."

"Faithful even unto death. And you, his brother, come to me now and, knowing all, dare to hold out to me the hope of forgiveness and of peace?" and the man stared incredulously into the kind, pitying eyes bent upon him.

"I, his brother, offer you now forgiveness of all your sins and peace which surpasseth all understanding."

The sick man was seized with a violent fit of coughing and when it had passed, he lay back in his chair exhausted, with closed eyes and white, pain-drawn face. The priest, wishing to give him a moment to rest and recover his breath, walked to the window and looked out. In the field below more than a score of ragged men, women and children were scratching and digging among piles of ashes, eagerly searching for and gathering up the half-burned cinders; searching, too, in the forlorn hope of finding something of greater value that might have been thrown away by accident. The rain beat noisily on the window pane and the priest shivered as he looked at those scantily-clad little children, not one of whom could boast of shoes and stockings, and at the white heads and bent figures of old women on whose unprotected shoulders the rain fell so pitilessly. What mattered the inclemency of the weather to them? Winter would be here by and by; they must gather in all the fuel possible before it was upon them with its snow and sleet and icy blasts. In fact, even when winter came, many of these same little children and old women, even grown men who either could not find other work to do or did not care to seek it, many of these same people would be seen day after day scratching and digging in this same field of ashes.

The priest turned from the window with a sigh of pity for the miserable creatures below. His glance strayed over the untidy kitchen which bore all the marks of the most extreme poverty and he gave another sigh of pity for the man who had been brought so low in the last days of his life, the man whom he had known in the time of his success and prosperity.

He approached the chair beside the stove and the tired eyes opened slowly and looked at him. Unaccustomed tears filled those eyes and the hard voice softened marvelously.

"Nancy was right," that changed voice was saying. "I am dying. Father, you say you bring me forgiveness in his name, forgiveness for the great wrong I did him. In his name, I will accept the gift. Father, I will confess my sins to you and beg God's pardon for them."

Two hours later, when poor, tired Maggie, with aching arms and aching back, returned from her day's work, she was surprised at the gentleness with which he greeted her. Never had he been so kind before: she was more accustomed to harsh words and even curses than kindness from him. She set about preparing their evening meal and he actually ate what she put before him without even once finding fault with the food or with her. She could not understand it and felt vaguely alarmed.

Again the door opened and a face peered in anxiously. It would look as if the owner of the face was fully prepared to slam the door and take to her heels at a second's notice. The man in the chair by the stove smiled faintly and called:

Isabel Cecilia Williams

"Come in, Nancy; it's all right."

The little stooped figure sidled into the room but stood with her hand upon the door ready for flight at any moment. She could not trust her eyes and ears, she knew they must be deceiving her.

"Come in, Nancy," the man repeated. "Come in and sit down there in the chair you occupied this afternoon when you dared to tell me the truth that all others feared to tell. You're a brave little woman, Nancy, and, thanks to you, all is well with me at last. As he said, he brought me forgiveness for my sins and peace which surpasseth all understanding. Thanks to you, Nancy, thanks to you."

"Thanks to me is it, lad? Not a bit of it, not a bit of it. Thanks be to God!" ejaculated Nancy fervently.

"Thanks be to God!" whispered Maggie, as a tear rolled down her worn and faded cheek and splashed into the pan of water in which she was washing the supper dishes. "Thanks be to God for bringin' him back even at the eleventh hour!"

THE STORY OF JULIE BENOIT

Julie leaned against the door of the room from which she had just been summoned. Her black eyes flashed defiance into the eyes of the woman watching her in sorrowful silence.

"Why you come here?" she cried. "Why you not leave me alone? I not want to see you nor anyone. You no right to come here; you not my forewoman now. You dismiss me in disgrace a week ago, you and that superintendent in your factory over there. What you come for; to punish me some more?"

"My poor child," returned the other gently, "you must not hate me so. Believe me, I love you, Julie, and I've come here as your friend."

"You a friend to me; me, Julie Benoit who is sent away from the factory because I steal all that money! No, no, I know better than that, you no friend to me, you despise me. All the girls point their finger at me, for I steal that money. But I give it all back, do I not? And the superintendent he say it is my first offense and he will not send me to prison. Oh yes! he is very kind. Julie have give back the money, Julie is forgiven, but she is a thief and cannot work with honest people. She must go, and without a reference. No one could recommend a thief. Well, Julie does go, so why you not let her alone?"

"Julie, Julie, listen to me," cried the forewoman almost in despair. "Believe it or not as you please, I have come here to-day to help you if I can. I have come because there was something in your face, a look in your eyes, that day you left us that has haunted me ever since. I have come because I feared you were in trouble and were too proud to tell us so. Julie, for twenty years I have been forewoman of my department over there in the factory. Many, many girls have worked with me, new ones coming, old ones going all the time. Some have left for one reason, some for another, but never before has one gone from me in anger or disgrace. All my girls have loved me, Julie, and I loved them. Why was it I never could win you, win your trust and confidence. Was I not kind to you, child? I tried to be for I wanted your love and trust."

The flashing eyes and angry face of the girl softened a little as the woman continued:

"I know you are not a bad girl, Julie. I know that you never before stole anything. I have been thinking of you all this week and worrying about you, for it must have been some great trouble which induced you to take that money. Why did you take it, child? Won't you please tell me?"

"You ask me why I take it? Well, I will tell you. Do you know what is in that room just behind this very door I lean against? It is my mother. She will never move again, never speak to me again; she is dead. Yes, she died last night but I not tell no one. If I tell, they will take her away and bury her I not know where. I have no money to bury her myself. Pretty soon I will have to tell, then they bury her in a pauper's grave with other people poor like us. I not know where they put her; I never can go and kneel at her grave and whisper to her that I have not forgotten.

"You want to know why I steal that money? Well, a week ago poor mother she is so very sick. They tell me she cannot live many days; but I think if only I have money I can save her yet. I can have doctors to see her, big doctors who will go to sick people only for very much money. I can buy her food and medicine and perhaps send her away to some place where the sun will shine for her, where she can breathe God's pure air. Why even strong people can scarce live in a place like this where the sunshine never come, where it is cold and damp all the time. How can the poor little mother hope to grow well again in such a place, without good food, often without a fire, the air not fit for anyone to breathe. I think of it all the time. I lie awake at night and think of it, it is before me all day at my work. Money, money, if only I have a little money, I can save my mother yet. Then the chance come, the money is there before me. I look at it, I take it. That is all.

"You ask me why I steal that money. I steal it for her, my mother; to save her life. Yes, and for her, too, the blind grandmother, and for them," and she pointed to a very old woman sitting close to the stove and holding in her arms a whimpering child of four. At her side crouched two more children, somewhat older, huddled together in a ragged shawl. They wore neither shoes nor stockings and the small feet were blue with cold.

"Oh, you poor child," exclaimed the forewoman, her eyes filling with tears. "Why did you not tell me a week ago instead of taking that money, for one wrong can never right another; why did you not tell me? We might not have been able to save your mother, but we could have helped you. Even after you took the money, if you had told me all, something might have been done for you. I wish you had told me, Julie, I wish you had told me."

The shocked grief of the woman's face and voice had their effect upon the girl, and it was in a much more gentle tone that she continued:

"You can see for yourself how it is with us now, but we are not always like this. If you care to listen and will sit down, I tell you all about it.

"No, indeed, we are not always like this. I can remember when father is alive how happy we all are. He is a mason, good and steady, and he work for us all the time. We live in a pretty little flat, it is bright and clean and mother keep it so and make everything look nice for us. She sing and she laugh and she look so pretty in those days. I go to school and Marie also, dear Marie who died one year ago. Antoine, too, he go to school with Marie and me. Lorraine there, she too little; she stay at home with mother and with grandmother.

"Well, we are all so happy until one day father is brought home to us. He is dead, killed at his work by a falling derrick. That same day poor little Baptiste, him there on grandmother's lap, he come into this cruel world. Mother is sick, so very sick for a long time after. It is weeks and weeks before she can walk around again. By the time she does, the little money she had saved is all gone; there is not a cent in the house and the landlord puts us out into the street.

"I am only twelve at the time but I go to work in a factory - not your factory, but one away off the other side of the river. I have to walk long, long distance in the cold, dark morning, and walk back again at night, but I am happy for I earn money to help at home. Mother she go to work too, in a great steam laundry where she stand all day at a big machine. She very thin and pale, and so tired at night she can hardly walk home. But she, too, is content; for she have work to do and work means money to buy food for the little ones and for the blind grandmother.

"We get along pretty well for almost three years. Then, just a year ago, the factory I work for shuts down. Times are hard, there is no more work for us, we must go. We do go. We try first one place, then another, to find work. It is the same story everywhere, times are hard and there is no work for us.

"Then mother gets that dreadful cold. The laundry where she works is always so very hot. She come out at night into the cold air; her coat is thin for she cannot buy a warm one and she get a dreadful chill one night as she comes home. She cough all the time after that. It shake her nearly all to pieces;

but she still go to her work till one day she fall beside her machine. They bring her home and we put her into bed and she never leave it again.

"What to do then we know not. One, two, three days pass; at last there is a day when grandmother and I eat nothing. We give the last scraps of bread to the children and spend the last two pennies on milk for mother. There is nothing left for us. We not sleep that night; we sit by the empty stove and we think all night. Grandmother is praying all the time; she is, oh so good, that grandmother. She pray and she pray, and she tell me God is kind and good, He will show us a way. Me, I am not good like that. I say to her God cannot be kind and merciful, or he would not treat us so. What have we done that He punish us like that? She say to me:

"'Hush, child, hush; you very bad, very wicked. God is good and kind and loving. He not try us any more than we can bear; He send us help soon if we trust in Him.'

"Next morning is cold, very cold; we have no fire and no food. I have been everywhere to look for work and find nothing. But I put on my hat to go out and try once more. Grandmother ask me what I do. I tell her I go again to look for work. She say: 'No, child, you stay here with your mother to-day; it is my turn now.'

"She is old; she is blind and I fear to have her go out alone, but she is firm and will go. She take her stick and she go out. She come back later with bread for the children and a little money to buy coal. I not ask her where she get it; I know. She beg it on the street. Every day she go out like that, and when she bring back food and money she not say one word and I not ask her where she get it; I know.

"She keeps us from starving for a few weeks and then, at last, I find work in your factory. For a time, I am almost happy again, for now grandmother need beg no more; my pay will keep us in food and fire. Even mother seems better for a little while, and I think perhaps she will get well and we will all be happy once again. But mother is soon very, very sick, and I see her dying day by day and can do nothing to help her.

"Then, that day last week, a party of ladies come to visit the factory. The wife of the superintendent is with them. She very handsome, very rich; she beautifully dressed. She stop near my table to take off her coat, the room is warm and the fur coat heavy. She lay her purse down on my table while she remove the garment; one of the ladies call to her and she go away, leaving the purse behind her on my table.

"Mother is very sick that morning; she not sleep all night, but cough, cough, cough. There is the purse before me. No one is looking; I pick it up and open it. It is filled with money, the money that may save my mother's life. That lady will never miss it. I slip the purse inside my dress and go on with my work. I can hardly keep from screaming with joy I am so happy to think I have the money which is going to save my mother's life. The ladies go away and I feel that I am safe; she has forget about her purse. I want to rush away at once, but I must stay at my work so no one will suspect.

"Presently the superintendent he come in and he talk to you and you look very grave. Then he say one of the ladies have left her purse on a table in this room. Will the girls be kind enough to stop work and search for it? He will give five dollars reward to the one who finds it. We all search but no purse is found, and he go away again. Pretty soon he come back and the lady with him. She look around for a few moments, then she walk straight over to my table. The superintendent ask is she sure, quite sure. She say she is perfectly sure. She lay her purse on that table in order to remove her coat, then forget to take it up again when she go away; and she look very hard at me.

"The superintendent ask me if I have seen the purse and I say no. I suppose he know by my face that I am lying for he tell you to take me to the dressing-room and search. Then I know there is no hope for me; if you search you find the purse, so I take it out and hand it to him. He talk to me about my wickedness but I not answer him. He discharge me, but I not say one word. You talk to me, but I not speak to you either, I am too heartbroken, too despairing. My mother she will die now, she will surely die; and grandmother she will have to go out begging once again.

"I come home and I tell them I am discharged. I not tell them why, for they very good and stealing is a sin. They be so shocked and sorry. I sit beside my mother, despair in my heart, and I watch her dying, dying, dying.

"Her pain is all over now; she leave me last night and she never come back again. I watch with her in there when you come. I watch with her some more when you go; then I must tell that she is gone, that she is dead, and they come and take her away," and she threw herself on the floor by the door of her mother's room in a perfect agony of grief.

In a moment the kind-hearted woman was on her knees beside the heartbroken girl, whom she gathered into her motherly arms, murmuring words of comfort all the while. Gradually the dreadful sobbing subsided, and after a time the girl was once more standing before that door she guarded so jealously. Seeing that she was her own calm self again, the forewoman said gently:

"My poor child, again I say that I wish you had told me a week ago. So much suffering would have been saved. However, this is no time for vain regrets, it is the time for action. I must leave you at once, Julie, but I will be back, and will, I hope, bring you good news. In the meantime do you say nothing to anyone about your mother. You will believe that I will help you? You will do as I say?"

"You very good," replied Julie simply, laying her hand in that of the forewoman; "when you want me, you find me there," and she pointed to the door behind which her mother's silent form was resting.

Two days later, the forewoman, seated at her desk, was apparently absorbed in the newspaper she was reading while leisurely disposing of her noonday lunch. In reality she was covertly watching an excited group of girls on the other side of the room who were discussing some matter of evident importance. Without doubt, something was wrong. The forewoman rather surmised what the trouble was and smiled behind the shelter of her newspaper. She knew these girls and was quite sure that the difficulty, whatever it was, would be brought to her for settlement. As she had said to Julie, she loved her girls, and they in turn loved and trusted her.

In this instance she had not long to wait. Presently the girls cast aside napkins and lunch boxes and moved toward the corner of the room where their forewoman was waiting. She watched their approach in smiling silence. Slightly in advance of the others came a small, impetuous figure, a painfully thin, cross-eyed girl of fifteen, whose abundant crop of freckles had earned for her the sobriquet of "Speckles." She had answered to that name for so long now that she had almost forgotten she ever owned any other. She was impulsive, good-hearted, and a general favorite in spite of her rather sharp little tongue. Rushing up to the forewoman's desk, she said excitedly:

"Miss Merton, it can't be true, what Louise has just been telling us, that you are going to let that horrid Julie Benoit come back again. You surely wouldn't take her back, would you, Miss Merton?"

"Yes, it is perfectly true," replied the forewoman calmly. "Julie will return to us next Monday, and I hope all my girls will do everything they can to make her feel that we are glad to have her back."

"But we're not glad. We don't want her back," cried one girl.

"Why it's impossible after what she did," added another.

"I, for one, wouldn't work in the same room with a girl like that," said a third, with a toss of her head. "I wouldn't dare leave any of my belongings out of my sight for a single instant."

"That's just the trouble," chimed several all at once. "We wouldn't feel safe for a moment knowing there was a thief amongst us."

During this outburst the forewoman sat quietly watching the indignant faces before her. Then she said very gravely:

"Girls, I think we all misjudged Julie, and really almost owe her an apology. I have asked her pardon, and though I do not expect you to do the same, I do ask you to receive her back with kindness."

"Misjudged her! Apology!" gasped Speckles. "She took that money, didn't she?"

"Yes."

"And a person who takes money that belongs to someone else is a thief, isn't she?"

"Yes, certainly."

"Well then, I say a thief is a thief, and I don't see where any misjudging comes in," and Speckles looked defiantly from one to another.

A tall blonde whose thoughtful blue eyes had been studying the forewoman's face, laid her hand on the excited girl's arm, remarking gently:

"Let's not judge too hastily, Speckles dear. I think Miss Merton has something to tell us. For my part I used to pity Julie, she seemed so weak and sickly and so terribly alone. She was with us but she was not one of us."

"Pity your grandmother," cried Speckles the irrepressible. "If she was alone all the time, it was her own fault. She was a stuck-up old thing and wouldn't make friends with any of us. If you'd speak to her she'd only stare at you with those fierce black eyes of hers and answer yes or no just as short and snappy as you please."

"I doubt if we tried very hard, any of us, to win her friendship, the poor little thing. And she did seem so forlorn and lonely at times," answered the blonde. "But there, girls, let's all keep quiet if we can for I know Miss Merton has something to tell us."

"You are right, Louise, I have a little story to tell you, the story of Julie Benoit," and she told them Julie's story as she had heard it from Julie herself. In conclusion, she added: "When I left that poor child beside her dead mother, I went at once to the superintendent and told him the whole story. You girls know how kind he is; many of you have had personal experience of his charity. He called in his wife and together they planned to bury Julie's mother as a Catholic should be buried, they to stand all the expense. They have also undertaken to see that the younger children are sent to school and the grandmother properly cared for, and Julie is to return to her place here on Monday.

"I wish you could have seen her face when I went back to those two dreadful rooms in the alley where she lives and told her what the superintendent and his wife had said. She stared at me, amazed, incredulous; then said slowly in an awed whisper:

"'They do all that for me, Julie Benoit the thief! You tell the lady it is I who steal her money but she forgive and have my mother buried like a Christian. She have her taken into church where the priest will bless her and pray over her. She have her buried where I can go and kneel beside her grave and tell her that I love her still and that I forget her never, no never. The lady do all that for me who steal her money. But she is good, she is kind to forgive me.'

"After a moment's thought, she added: 'You think God will forgive me too? I very bad, very wicked; I say all those dreadful things about Him, but He will forgive me, is it not so? Grandmother say He good and kind. You think He will forgive me if I ask Him?'

"It was a very different Julie that I left that night; oh! very different from the girl who met me with such fierceness earlier in the evening. Just as I was leaving, she said to me very humbly: 'The girls at the factory, you think they will forgive me also? I very rude to them; I say I hate them all. You think they will forgive me?'

"So now, my girls, your welcome to Julie on Monday morning will be the best answer to that question."

"Will we forgive her, the poor girl!" cried Speckles impulsively. "You bet we will. If there's any one here who won't be kind to that poor little Julie, she'll just have to reckon with me. I think it is we who should ask her to forgive us, for I must admit we were all rather hateful to her. Oh, I say, girls! I've just got an idea," she continued. "Here, Louise, just hand me one of those empty boxes from that shelf over your head. There you are. Now then, this is a hat and I pass it around to each of you, so. I say to each one of you: 'Did you notice that poor Julie has been wearing a thin summer coat all this bitter winter weather? It used to make me shiver just to look at her. Did any of you notice that her shoes were all broken through and even in rain or snow storms she never had any rubbers to wear over them?' Suppose each one of us chip in a few pennies, we can all spare a little, and have Miss Merton give it to her to buy shoes or something for herself. I'll start with fifty cents."

The box was passed from one to another, each contributing what she could, and each contribution meaning more or less of a sacrifice to the donor. In this way a goodly sum was collected and laid on Miss Merton's table.

"There, girls," said the triumphant Speckles. "That will show

Julie whether we have forgiven her or not. And now, do you hear that musical whistle calling us back to our places? We'd better hustle for the machines will start up in a minute or two. Machines are like time and the tide, they wait for no man. Nor woman, either, not even for Julie Benoit," and with a laugh, Speckles was off like the wind.

As the girls departed, each to her own machine or work-table, Miss Merton looked after them, a tear in her eye and a smile upon her lips.

"God bless my girls," she said to herself. "Their hearts are in the right place, every one of them. I need have no fear of the welcome they will give my poor little Julie Benoit."

PETER

Peter was thinking. Not that it was an unusual event for Peter to think. Quite the contrary! To Peter himself it seemed that life was one continuous round of thinking and planning and worrying. It certainly was for him, especially since the advent of the baby, that wonderful baby sister of his. Somehow things had not mattered so much before, when there was no one to be considered but himself. Now it was different, with his baby to be thought of and cared for. Peter was worried and anxious. He felt that a great responsibility rested upon his shoulders. They were young shoulders, too, far too young to be burdened with the cares and troubles of life.

The winter wind came tearing down the street, stinging his face and piercing through his thin garments. Shivering, he turned up the collar of his worn and ragged coat and thrust his hands deep into the pockets. Then he hastened on with eyes on the ground and bent down head, for Peter was thinking. A mighty problem confronted him, a problem which must be solved at once.

He turned into the dirty, narrow alley in which he lived, opened the door of a tenement house, and, running quickly up a flight of stairs, entered Mrs. Dempsey's kitchen. The savory odor of frying ham greeted his nostrils and reminded him that he had had nothing to eat since morning. Well, never mind that, he would have supper soon now, he and baby together.

"Bless me, Peter, is that you home so early?" cried cheery Mrs.

Isabel Cecilia Williams

Dempsey turning around from the stove, frying-pan in one hand, a large fork in the other. "You must have had good luck to-night to be back so early."

Peter caught up in his arms the pretty child who toddled across the floor and threw herself upon him with a shriek of delight. With a gravity befitting his great responsibility, he seated himself upon a nearby chair, holding the baby close to him and smoothing back the tangled yellow curls.

"Yes, Mrs. Dempsey, I had real good luck to-night. Was all sold out long afore the other fellers, then hustled right home to baby. I hope she wasn't no bother to ye, Mrs. Dempsey."

"Bother is it? The darlin', an' she as quiet as a little lamb. It's an angel she is entirely an' ye'd think so yerself if ye could have seen the nice supper of bread and milk she ate along with my own young ones."

"Does angels eat bread and milk, Mrs. Dempsey?" Peter asked the question in all sincerity. He had often wondered about angels and he really wanted to know.

"Oh, I guess they does," replied the good woman absently, too busy with her cooking to pay much heed to what Peter was saying. "Goin', Peter? Wish ye could stay and have a bite yerself, but I suppose if that precious father of your'n come home and his supper warn't ready he'd make it pretty hot for you, poor child. Well, good-night, Peter. Bring the baby back in the morning."

"By the way, Peter," she called after him just as he was closing the door. "To-morrow's Christmas day ye know. Don't forget to drop into the church on yer way home and hear Mass, like a good boy."

Peter's ideas on the subject of religion were very vague. Mrs. Dempsey had told him he must always attend Mass on Sunday and reminded him of the fact every Saturday night when he would come to claim the baby. Perhaps Christmas was another sort of Sunday, thought Peter. To him Christmas had always meant a time when other boys and girls talked of nothing but Christmas trees and turkey and wonderful presents they had received. No one had ever given Peter anything. He wondered if Mrs. Dempsey would. He had not known Mrs. Dempsey last Christmas; she came to the alley only a few months ago. Life had been somewhat easier for Peter since her coming for she helped so much in caring for baby while he was out. He wished Mrs. Dempsey would give baby something for Christmas. He had hoped to do so himself, but somehow he never could find a cent for anything except the absolute necessities of life. Sometimes he could do no more than provide bread and milk for the baby and go hungry himself. That was when father would beat him and take away the few pennies he was saving to buy food for the little sister and himself.

With baby held carefully in his arms, Peter descended the two flights of stairs to his home in the cellar. As he pushed open the door of the room which served as kitchen and living room in the daytime and as sleeping apartment for himself and baby at night, the damp chill of the place struck him as it never had done before. Groping his way to the table he lighted the candle upon it. Then, after wrapping baby in his mother's old shawl and depositing her upon their bed in the corner, he proceeded to make a fire in the cracked and rusty stove. Peter was only eleven, but the children of the slums are little men and women almost from their cradles, and Peter was really the man of the family. He it was who cared for the baby and prepared their frugal meals; he it was who cried his papers upon the street in the cold darkness of the winter mornings, who ran errands all day for the grocer on the next corner and again in the evening sallied forth with his papers under his arm in order to procure food to keep the life in their bodies. If father ever earned any money but little of it was contributed to the family support.

As Peter wrestled with the fire, which positively refused to kindle, he was still revolving in his mind the problem which troubled him. He had been thinking of it all day, and the only thing he could decide was that something must be done at once, but what that something was to be he could not imagine. Things had been going from bad to worse lately, and after last night he would never know an easy moment while baby was under the same roof with father and mother. For himself he did not care. He had grown accustomed to the beatings, to the drunken quarrels and fearful language; in fact, he had never known anything different. But last night father had tried to hurt baby. He might try again and perhaps next time no Peter would be at hand to save her. They were unusually bad last night, both father and mother; the child was frightened and had begun to whimper. Angered still further by the sound, the man had seized a stove-lifter and flung it straight at baby's head. But Peter had already sprung between and the missile struck him full on the forehead, causing a wicked-looking bruise. He had lain stunned for a time, then crept into bed with baby and listened in terror as the quarrel between his father and mother progressed from words to blows. He had not minded these things before, but what would he do if father should ever beat baby as he, Peter, had been beaten so many times? And Peter felt the time was coming when father would surely do it. Last night was but the beginning.

A noise from the next room told him that mother must be waking from the drunken sleep in which she had lain for several hours. At any moment she might open that door and enter the kitchen, and her temper was always terrible when she would first awaken from those long sleeps which followed a carousal. In a few moments, too, father would come home. The fire refused to burn; so supper would not be ready, and with mother in a temper and no supper at hand, something would surely happen.

Peter looked at the sleeping baby and shuddered. For her sake he dared not face another night like last night. Yet, what could he do? A volley of imprecations from the next room decided him: he must take baby away from here and at once. Yes, he would take her away, but where, where could he go? Where in all the great city could he find a shelter for his baby on this cold winter night? If he did take her away it might be only to have her freeze to death on the street. Well, they must go, anyway. No matter what happened to them later they must leave here at once.

Rearranging the shawl so that part of it covered the golden head, he stooped and gathered the baby into his arms. Then it all came to him in a sudden flash of inspiration and he almost laughed aloud in his joy as he hurried from the room and out into the street. He knew exactly where to go and wondered why he had not thought of it before. How foolish he had been not to think of it at once!

One day last summer he had stood outside a tall iron railing and watched a crowd of happy children at play in the grounds which the railing enclosed. He could see it all now, the yard, the romping children and the great brick building on the other side of that railing through which he watched enviously. They were having such a good time, he did wish he might go in and join in the fun. But he could not spare the time, he had wasted too much already, and the grocer would scold him for being so long on the errand which had brought him into the neighborhood of the yard and the children. As he turned reluctantly away, two ladies passed and he heard one say in answer to a question from her companion:

"That building? Why, that is St. Teresa's Orphanage, a home for poor children who have no parents or else have bad ones who neglect or ill treat them. The good sisters gather in all such needy children whom they can find, care for them, educate them and teach them a trade so that they may - "

The rest Peter had not heard, but those few words, spoken by the passing lady on that day last summer, had suddenly recurred to his mind. "St. Teresa's Orphanage, a home for children with bad parents who neglect or ill treat them." That was their case exactly, baby's and his. To St. Teresa's, then, they must go in search of a home. He was quite sure he could find it again. It was ever so far away, over on the other side of the city, but he remembered the way perfectly, and would have no difficulty in reaching the orphanage.

For some time Peter trudged bravely along the city streets. It was quite dark now and lights streamed from the windows of shops and houses as he passed. Throngs of people hurried by anxious to escape from the cold night to the firesides of home. All these people carried mysterious-looking parcels; "Christmas presents for some happy little boy or girl," thought Peter. Twice he stopped to shift the baby from one shoulder to the other. He never knew before that she was so heavy; his half frozen little arms almost refused to carry their burden any longer. He was terribly tired, and he wondered why the lights were dancing so. They were turning round and round and made him so dizzy he could scarce see where he was going. He did not think, that day last summer, that the way was quite so long as this. Surely, he must have been walking for hours and hours. Oh! why was baby so heavy and why would those lights persist in dancing so?

He wondered if they could be lost and what would happen to them if they were. He was almost certain he had taken the right turnings every time, but he might have made a mistake. At that last corner he was not quite sure whether he should turn to the left or the right. If they were lost, what would become of them?

The lights were acting very strangely to-night; they had stopped dancing now but were all turning black, and what was this funny feeling that was creeping over him? He sat down hurriedly on some steps he was passing and leaned his head against the railing for support. He felt baby slipping from his arms onto the step beside him but was powerless to hold her. Once more that funny feeling was creeping over him and he wondered if he could be dying. Mr. Dempsey's Tim had died. Peter had gone upstairs to see him. They had put him into a funny-looking white box that was nearly covered with flowers, and he looked so strange lying there all white and still among the blossoms. The next day the white box, the flowers and poor little Tim were carried away. The neighbors said Tim was dead; Mrs. Dempsey said he had gone to heaven. Peter wondered if he died would anyone put him in a white box and cover him with flowers; if he died, would he go to heaven and see Tim there?

Peter had often been very anxious as to what heaven was like. He had asked Mrs. Dempsey. Her answer had not been quite satisfactory, but then she could not know exactly since she had never been there. And the angels, what were they like? Again Mrs. Dempsey had been referred to and again the reply was most disappointing. Beautiful beings with wings? Why, birds had wings and some of them were very beautiful. As for singing before the throne of God; well, Peter could not even guess what the throne of God meant.

He guessed he must be dying; he felt dead already, all except his head. That would go soon and then he would see the angels he had wondered so much about. But if he died, what would become of baby? Who would look after his precious baby? That dreadful thought caused him to open his eyes suddenly. With a great effort he raised his head and the sight of the iron railing against which he was leaning made his heart bound with a sudden thrill of hope and put new life into the exhausted little frame. It was the railing through which he had watched the children on that day last summer, and the steps on which he sat were the steps of St. Teresa's Orphanage. He had taken the right turning after all and had reached his destination without knowing it.

With difficulty. Peter got upon his feet, lifted the baby and essayed to drag himself up that long flight of steps. Panting, exhausted, he reached the top and laid his burden down at the threshold of that door which always opened so gladly to receive such waifs as he. In the darkness Peter felt around for the bell. Surely, there must be a bell somewhere. He must find it quickly for that dreadful feeling was creeping over him and he knew in another moment he would fall. Where was it; oh! why could he not find it? At last the despairing fingers touched the button of an electric bell; they pressed it hard, and a loud peal rang through the hall inside. Then Peter sank down to the ground beside the baby and even his head went this time.

A moment later (or so it seemed to Peter) he opened his eyes and saw bending over him the most beautiful face he had ever beheld. He knew now that he was in heaven was looking on the face of an angel. It was just what he should think an angel's face ought to be, so sweet and kind and gentle, the soft eyes filled with heavenly love and pity. And there were the wings, too, all white and shining, but Mrs. Dempsey had neglected to mention that angels' wings grew out of their heads. Somehow, Peter had supposed their wings grew from their shoulders; he was sure Mrs. Dempsey had said so. He would like to send her a message and tell her how mistaken she had been. He wondered if he could.

He felt a gentle hand slip beneath his shoulders and raise him a little and the angel commenced to feed him with something warm and sweet upon a spoon. It tasted better than anything he had ever eaten before.

Suddenly he thought of baby. What had happened to her? Was she in heaven too? He tried to ask the angel, but found he could not utter a word; he was too weak and tired. The kind eyes watching him interpreted rightly the anxious look that crossed his face; they were well accustomed to divining the unspoken troubles of worried little minds. The angel spoke and to Peter the voice sounded like heavenly music:

"You must not try to talk, dear. Just finish this gruel like a good boy and then go to sleep again. Your baby sister is quite safe, and is sleeping sweetly in her crib over in the little one's dormitory. You shall see her in the morning if you are good now and do as I tell you."

As he finished the gruel his eyes closed wearily for a moment, and when he opened them again there were two angels leaning over him. The second was not nearly so lovely as the first, but her face, too, bore that same look of heavenly sweetness which Peter felt instinctively none but angels' faces could wear. It was the look which older people than Peter have often marveled at; the look one sees upon the faces of those who have died to the world and to themselves and given their entire being to God in a life of charity and self-sacrifice.

The second angel laid her fingers on his wrist and seemed to be counting something as she kept her eyes on a small silver watch she held in her hand. Then she poured a spoonful of bright-colored liquid from a bottle, and, lifting his head, bade him swallow the medicine. Unquestioningly he obeyed, and as his head was laid back upon the pillow he felt himself slipping away into the land of oblivion. Just as consciousness was leaving him, he heard a voice, seemingly far away, saying:

"He will do very nicely now, Sister Agnes. It was simply a case of starvation and complete exhaustion."

Vaguely he wondered what she meant.

GOD'S WAY

"We have reached the summit at last, Cecile? The hill seemed unusually steep to-night and the way unusually long."

"Yes, mother, we have reached the top at last and here is the rustic bench on which we usually sit and watch the sun go down behind those blue and misty hills in the distance."

"Ah! those hills, Cecile. How I have always loved them. To me this has ever seemed the fairest spot on earth, and the view from this hill just at sunset the most beautiful I have ever seen. It is ten long years since my eyes have beheld it, but in my mind I still see it all so clearly. Tell me it is all there, Cecile, just as it was on that evening so many, many years ago when I first looked upon its beauties. Your dear father had just brought me, a happy bride, here to his northern home. We walked up the hill together to watch the sun set and I thought then I had never seen a lovelier view: the green fields of waving corn, and the apple orchards all in blossom, sloping down gradually to the river; the river itself tumbling and tossing madly over the waterfall far up there to the left, then swirling and eddying on for a space, only to grow calm once more quietly, steadily, resume its placid journey to the ocean. Beyond the river, those wonderful forests, dark, mysterious and silent. They rise and rise, higher, ever higher, and terminate at last in the blue and misty hills of which you were just speaking. I love it all, Cecile, and I could not bear to think that any part of it had changed with the advancing years. Tell me it is just the same; tell me it is all there as it was so long ago."

"Yes, mother dear," answered the younger woman, "it is all there just as it has ever been; the fields and the river, the forests and the hills beyond."

Cecile neglected to mention that the fields were now mere barren stubble and that the river was visible only here and there as it peeped through between the many buildings lining its banks; immense buildings of factory and mill, smaller structures, cottages and tenement houses occupied by the workers in factory and mill. She supposed the forests were still there but the day had been very sultry with scarce a breath of air stirring and a heavy pall of smoke from the huge chimneys hung over the valley, hiding everything which lay beyond. Only the tops of the distant hills rose in triumph above it.

"I am glad to think it is all unchanged," said the mother with a sigh of content. "I know it is foolish to feel as I do about it, but it would be a real grief to me to think that my beautiful valley had been sacrificed to the need or the greed of advancing civilization."

"God has been very good to me, Cecile, and I thank Him with all my heart for the blessings He has sent me to compensate for that one dreadful calamity, your dear father's sudden death ten years ago and my long illness and subsequent blindness. As I sat to-day in my little garden listening to the twittering of the birds, and inhaling the fragrance of my flowers, I was thinking how peaceful and happy my life is and how grateful I should be. You know, dear, just occasionally I long to be able to see again, to see the birds and the flowers, to see the beautiful world around me. That is very wrong and wicked I know, and I chase the rebellious wish away by thinking of my many blessings, especially of you and my Philippe. You have both been my comfort and consolation. By the way, dear, no letter has come from Philippe to-day?"

"No, mother, not yet."

"It is strange that we have not heard from him. This is the first time he has not written to me for my birthday."

"But he did not forget you, mother. Are you not wearing his beautiful gift to you which arrived this morning?"

"No, he did not forget," replied the older woman, as her fingers strayed lovingly over the lace scarf resting so lightly on her snow-white hair. "My Philippe never forgets and that is why I worried just a little this morning when his usual birthday letter did not come. Then, this afternoon, a sudden idea occurred to me which made me very happy. Shall I tell you what it was, Cecile? I am quite sure I have discovered the reason why Philippe did not write me for my birthday."

It was well the blind eyes could not see the look of startled fear which flashed across Cecile's face.

"You have discovered why he did not write?" she exclaimed, and her voice trembled slightly.

The mother laughed happily. "Yes, I am quite sure I have discovered the reason. I have a feeling, and I know it is a true feeling, that before my birthday is quite over Philippe will be here with us. He is coming, Cecile; he is not far away at this very moment, and before the evening is over he will be with us."

Tears filled Cecile's eyes but she rose quietly and said, trying to speak lightly:

"The night mist is rising from the river, mother dear. Had we not better turn our faces toward the east and home?"

"You are right, child, it will be as well for us to go home a little early to-night. I am feeling unaccountably weary though very, very happy. It will be best for me to go home and rest a little before the evening train arrives bringing my Philippe back to me."

Cecile said nothing, but very gently, very tenderly guided the blind mother's steps as they wended their way homeward in the sweet summer twilight.

Half an hour later Cecile paced restlessly up and down the broad veranda of her home. She had left her mother sleeping on the couch in her pretty sitting-room upstairs and could now face the problems and difficulties which confronted her. In her mind she reviewed the years that had come and gone since that sad night when her dying father had whispered almost with his last breath:

"Your mother, Cecile; I trust her to you. Take care of her for me when I am no longer here to watch over her myself. Promise me you will shield her from every worry, that you will stand between her and all troubles as I have always done."

The girl had promised and right faithfully had she kept her word, but at what a cost to herself! She was thinking now of her promise and of how she had kept it. She was thinking, too, of her mother's serious illness which had followed that night, an illness from which she had recovered, it is true, but which left her blind for life. What a terrible calamity her mother's blindness had appeared to be at that time, and yet, there came a day, that dreadful day two years ago, when she had thanked God on her knees for the affliction which enabled her to conceal the trouble which had come upon them.

Once more she lived through that day two years ago, the day when those awful letters had come, one from Philippe, one from the lawyers. She had read them at first without comprehending their meaning. Then as the truth began to dawn upon her, she cried to herself that it could not be true, it could not be. There was some terrible mistake somewhere. But there it was before her in black and white; Philippe's own confession, the lawyers' letter confirming all the facts. They were ruined, penniless, and Philippe had done this thing; Philippe, her tall handsome brother, the pride and darling of their mother's heart. But worse than poverty, worse than ruin faced them. Philippe was a disgraced man, sentenced to jail for fifteen years.

It was an old, old story; she had heard of such cases before but paid little heed to them. Now it was Philippe, her brother, and oh! how different it all seemed. It was simply the story of an ambitious young man, making his way in the world, winning name and fame among the ablest financiers of the Western city in which he had elected to live his life. It was simply the story of one who had much and who wanted more, who strained every nerve to win in the great game he was playing, the game of money-getting. It was the story of one who risked all in one grand final coup, who risked all and lost all. And what was risked and lost was not his alone; everything belonging to his mother and sister had gone too. Worse still, he had made use of money which was not theirs, funds of the bank of which he was treasurer. Of course, he had only borrowed them, he had been so sure of success, and he intended replacing the money in a few days. He had reasoned as so many men before him had reasoned, as men will continue to reason as long as this world shall be.

Such had been the trial which faced Cecile that day two years ago. Her one thought had been that mother must never know; her heart had always been weak and the shock would kill her, simply kill her. Words her mother had once spoken to her returned to her mind as she had finished reading those letters. The remark had been caused by some little act of thoughtfulness on Philippe's part, some little gift he had sent her, for Philippe had always been careful to remember all the little household feast days with beautiful and often costly gifts.

"Cecile," her mother had said, "you have both been good children to me, you and Philippe, good and kind and thoughtful. I think it would break my heart if my children should ever forget me, ever cease to love me. I can imagine but one thing worse, to have them forget their God, to know that they had committed any grievous wrong. I have sometimes heard of mothers whose sons have been led astray into ways of wickedness and proved a disgrace to themselves and to their families, and I have said to myself: 'Poor woman, how can she bear it, how can she go on living knowing what her boy has become? It would kill me, I know it would. Thank God, my Philippe is a good boy, brave and upright like his father; I shall never have cause to worry about him.'"

Those words kept ringing through Cecile's brain as she had read the letters over, and over again, and she had determined then and there, at all costs, her mother should never know. But how was she going to conceal the fact of their poverty, of their absolute ruin?

They had always lived in comfort and where was she to find the money to supply their daily needs? Since her father's death and her mother's affliction, they had lived in the utmost seclusion. The few friends of her earlier life had drifted away one by one and there was no one to whom she could turn for help or advice in her hour of need. She must manage alone somehow, she and faithful black Mandy to whom her mother was still the "li'l Missy" of long years ago, the "l'il Missy" of the happy days on the southern plantation.

For two years they had succeeded, but by what sacrifices to themselves no one would ever know. Many a time they had been reduced almost to the verge of starvation in order to provide for the blind mother the little delicacies to which she had been accustomed. Gradually, articles of furniture disapp-eared from their accustomed places; costly pieces of bric-a-brac, rare old china, everything of value which Cecile thought her mother would not be likely to miss. Cecile's own apart-ment had been reduced to four walls, a bare floor, one chair and the bed upon which she slept. The mother's rooms and Philippe's alone remained untouched.

Then Cecile found employment in the office of one of those new factories which had recently been erected over there beyond the town. This step had been the cause of the first disagreement between her mother and herself.

"Why, Cecile, what do you mean?" the poor mother had gasped in her utter bewilderment when informed of her daughter's intention. "Surely, I misunderstood what you just said. Bookkeeper in the office of a *factory*! Earn your own living! What *are* you talking about! What strange jest is this, my dear? For you certainly cannot be in earnest."

"Indeed I am not jesting, mother dear, but am very much in earnest. I really want to earn money of my own, and shall be so much happier if I have a regular occupation. And you want me to be happy, do you not?"

"I cannot understand you at all, Cecile. I really cannot. In my youth, we of the south considered it a disgrace for a young lady to even dream of earning her living. Your father left us plenty of money. I do not know just how it was invested, for I never cared to trouble my head about money matters. I preferred to leave all that to you and the lawyers. Still, I know my income is quite sufficient for our wants. Even if we should lose our money, there is Philippe to provide for us. He would agree with me, I know. He would never, never allow his sister to work for a living."

Of course Cecile had persisted in her resolution, and it grieved her to feel that her mother had never become reconciled to what she considered a mere whim.

Letters from Philippe came at occasional intervals, letters which were carefully edited before she read them aloud to her mother. Gifts from Philippe came too, just as they had always done, but now each gift meant some added sacrifice for poor Cecile. Her very last bit of jewelry, a gift from her father on the Christmas before he died, had been sold to purchase the lace scarf which had come that morning in Philippe's name.

Of all this Cecile was thinking as she paced the veranda that summer night. It had all been very hard to bear but it was as nothing compared with that last blow which had fallen two nights ago.

She had been to the town for necessary supplies and was returning rather late in the evening. The road was lonely, deserted, and she could not suppress the cry of fright which rose to her lips as a man sprang from a little thicket which she was passing and stood directly before her, barring her path. Her second cry was one, not of fear, but of startled recognition. The man was Philippe, no longer her handsome Philippe, but a ragged, wild-eyed, desperate man. His story was told in a few words. He had grown restive under the confinement of prison life, then frantic, simply frantic, and had made up his mind to escape. How, he did not know, but he schemed and planned and watched his chance and finally succeeded in getting away. He had managed to make his way to her, and now she must give him money to enable him to get out of the country.

Money? Where was she to find money to give him?

"But you must, Cecile; you must give me every cent you can lay hands on," he had cried savagely. "They are after me, I tell you, and if I am taken back it will be to answer to a charge of murder. Of course, I didn't mean it, you understand. One of the guards was in my way, and - well, there's one guard less in the world, that's all."

He had come to the house late that night and she had given him food, some of his own clothes which still hung in his room and which the mother had never allowed anyone to touch, and all the money she "could lay hands on." It was not much but it was every cent she had. She had heard nothing from him since, and the suspense of the last two days had been agonizing, the alternate hopes and fears, the wondering, wondering where he was, what was happening to him at that very moment.

The click of the garden gate and a footstep upon the gravel walk caused her to turn hastily and descend the veranda steps. At first, she thought it was Philippe come back to her, but a second glance showed that the figure approaching through the dusk was that of good Father Anselm, her parish priest. He was a young man, only recently appointed to the town, but he knew her story and had frequently helped her with kindly advice and sympathy. Her heart stood still as she watched his approach. Something in his manner, something in his face seen dimly through the gathering darkness, told her that he was the bearer of evil tidings.

"What is it, Father?" she asked tremulously. "Is it that they have taken him?"

"Yes, my child, they have taken him. They are bringing him here."

"Bringing him here! But why, why should they bring him here?" A sudden dreadful thought flashed through her mind. "Father, you have not told me all; there is something else."

"My poor child, there *is* something else to tell you."

"You need not tell it, Father, I know. They have taken him, but not - alive. My poor Philippe is gone, dead. Tell me how it happened, Father, will you please?"

The girl's unnatural calm was more pitiful than any outburst of grief could have been, and an immeasurable compassion spoke in the priest's voice as he told the story of Philippe's death.

"He was hiding in the deserted hut in Planter's Wood (you know the spot, Cecile) and they discovered his place of concealment. They had been following after him for days but he thought he would be safe there and could come out at night and procure food from you. There was a short, sharp struggle in which he received a mortal wound. Doctors were sent for; I, too, was summoned. Thank God, he was conscious up to the very last and I arrived in time to reconcile him with the Master whose love he had outraged, whose commands he had broken. His end was very quiet and peaceful, he simply closed his eyes and fell asleep as a little baby might.

"But we must not stand here talking, my child. We have a duty to perform, you and I, and we must be brave and perform that duty at once, difficult though it may be. Where is your mother, Cecile? She will have to be told before - before they arrive. I came on ahead for that very purpose."

"We cannot tell her, Father, we cannot. It will kill her."

"We *must* tell her; it will be impossible to hide it. Take me to her and we will tell her together. God will be with us and will help us, my child."

"Oh! if God would only spare her, if He would only spare her! If He would only open a way so we need not tell her!"

Her brain was in a whirl as she mounted the stairs; she was stunned, broken. Of one thing only was she perfectly conscious. Philippe was coming and his mother must be awakened. That mother's last words as she had closed her eyes were:

"I am strangely weary, Cecile, weary and very drowsy. I think I shall sleep a little, but be sure and wake me when Philippe comes."

Wake her when Philippe comes! Yes, for Philippe *is* coming and his mother must be wakened.

They stood beside the couch and looked down upon the sleeping woman. How quietly she rested there, how still she was and peaceful! But how *very* still she was, and what was that scarcely palpable shadow resting on the sweet, calm face? Was it only a shade cast by the lamp which Cecile had brought in and placed upon a table behind them, or was it - ?

With a cry of alarm, the girl fell on her knees and caught frantically at her mother's hand. It lay in hers absolutely passive and cold, so cold. The priest raised the lamp till the light shone full upon the face of the sleeper. Sleeping she was indeed, the last long sleep from which not they, not Philippe, not anyone could waken her.

Father Anselm laid his hand on the head of the stricken girl and said gently:

"A moment ago, my child, you prayed that God might spare her. He had granted your prayer even before it was uttered. We need not tell her now for she has learned it all from One who could tell it far more gently, far more mercifully than we could."

The sound of shuffling steps, as of men who carried a heavy burden, came up to them from the gravel walk below.

"Requiescant in pace," whispered the priest.

Cecile knelt as if turned to stone. Mechanically, she listened to the voice of the priest reciting the De Profundis; she listened to the call of the crickets shrilling through the summer night without; she listened to the heart-breaking sobs of faithful black Mandy crouching on the floor by the side of her "li'l Missy;" she listened to those shuffling footsteps as they entered the house, slowly mounted the staircase and paused at the door of what had once been Philippe's room.

Yet again the priest's voice recited:

"Requiescant in pace."

And this time, Cecile, laying her cheek upon the dear cold hand she held in hers, responded brokenly:

"Amen."

Choose from Thousands of 1stWorldLibrary Classics By

A. M. Barnard
Ada Leverson
Adolphus William Ward
Aesop
Agatha Christie
Alexander Aaronsohn
Alexander Kielland
Alexandre Dumas
Alfred Gatty
Alfred Ollivant
Alice Duer Miller
Alice Turner Curtis
Alice Dunbar
Allen Chapman
Ambrose Bierce
Amelia E. Barr
Amory H. Bradford
Andrew Lang
Andrew McFarland Davis
Andy Adams
Anna Alice Chapin
Anna Sewell
Annie Besant
Annie Hamilton Donnell
Annie Payson Call
Annie Roe Carr
Annonaymous
Anton Chekhov
Arnold Bennett
Arthur Conan Doyle
Arthur M. Winfield
Arthur Ransome
Arthur Schnitzler
Atticus
B.H. Baden-Powell
B. M. Bower
B. C. Chatterjee
Baroness Emmuska Orczy
Baroness Orczy
Basil King
Bayard Taylor
Ben Macomber
Bertha Muzzy Bower
Bjornstjerne Bjorson
Booth Tarkington
Boyd Cable
Bram Stoker
C. Collodi
C. E. Orr

C. M. Ingleby
Carolyn Wells
Catherine Parr Traill
Charles A. Eastman
Charles Amory Beach
Charles Dickens
Charles Dudley Warner
Charles Farrar Browne
Charles Ives
Charles Kingsley
Charles Klein
Charles Hanson Towne
Charles Lathrop Pack
Charles Romyn Dake
Charles Whibley
Charles Willing Beale
Charlotte M. Braeme
Charlotte M. Yonge
Charlotte Perkins Stetson
Clair W. Hayes
Clarence Day Jr.
Clarence E. Mulford
Clemence Housman
Confucius
Coningsby Dawson
Cornelis DeWitt Wilcox
Cyril Burleigh
D. H. Lawrence
Daniel Defoe
David Garnett
Dinah Craik
Don Carlos Janes
Donald Keyhoe
Dorothy Kilner
Dougan Clark
Douglas Fairbanks
E. Nesbit
E.P.Roe
E. Phillips Oppenheim
Earl Barnes
Edgar Rice Burroughs
Edith Van Dyne
Edith Wharton
Edward Everett Hale
Edward J. O'Biren
Edward S. Ellis
Edwin L. Arnold
Eleanor Atkins
Eliot Gregory

Elizabeth Gaskell
Elizabeth McCracken
Elizabeth Von Arnim
Ellem Key
Emerson Hough
Emilie F. Carlen
Emily Dickinson
Enid Bagnold
Enilor Macartney Lane
Erasmus W. Jones
Ernie Howard Pie
Ethel May Dell
Ethel Turner
Ethel Watts Mumford
Eugenie Foa
Eugene Wood
Eustace Hale Ball
Evelyn Everett-green
Everard Cotes
F. H. Cheley
F. J. Cross
F. Marion Crawford
Federick Austin Ogg
Ferdinand Ossendowski
Francis Bacon
Francis Darwin
Frances Hodgson Burnett
Frances Parkinson Keyes
Frank Gee Patchin
Frank Harris
Frank Jewett Mather
Frank L. Packard
Frank V. Webster
Frederic Stewart Isham
Frederick Trevor Hill
Frederick Winslow Taylor
Friedrich Kerst
Friedrich Nietzsche
Fyodor Dostoyevsky
G.A. Henty
G.K. Chesterton
Gabrielle E. Jackson
Garrett P. Serviss
Gaston Leroux
George A. Warren
George Ade
Geroge Bernard Shaw
George Durston
George Ebers

George Eliot
George Gissing
George MacDonald
George Meredith
George Orwell
George Sylvester Viereck
George Tucker
George W. Cable
George Wharton James
Gertrude Atherton
Gordon Casserly
Grace E. King
Grace Gallatin
Grace Greenwood
Grant Allen
Guillermo A. Sherwell
Gulielma Zollinger
Gustav Flaubert
H. A. Cody
H. B. Irving
H.C. Bailey
H. G. Wells
H. H. Munro
H. Irving Hancock
H. Rider Haggard
H. W. C. Davis
Haldeman Julius
Hall Caine
Hamilton Wright Mabie
Hans Christian Andersen
Harold Avery
Harold McGrath
Harriet Beecher Stowe
Harry Castlemon
Harry Coghill
Harry Houidini
Hayden Carruth
Helent Hunt Jackson
Helen Nicolay
Hendrik Conscience
Hendy David Thoreau
Henri Barbusse
Henrik Ibsen
Henry Adams
Henry Ford
Henry Frost
Henry James
Henry Jones Ford
Henry Seton Merriman
Henry W Longfellow
Herbert A. Giles

Herbert Carter
Herbert N. Casson
Herman Hesse
Hildegard G. Frey
Homer
Honore De Balzac
Horace B. Day
Horace Walpole
Horatio Alger Jr.
Howard Pyle
Howard R. Garis
Hugh Lofting
Hugh Walpole
Humphry Ward
Ian Maclaren
Inez Haynes Gillmore
Irving Bacheller
Isabel Hornibrook
Israel Abrahams
Ivan Turgenev
J.G.Austin
J. Henri Fabre
J. M. Barrie
J. Macdonald Oxley
J. S. Fletcher
J. S. Knowles
J. Storer Clouston
Jack London
Jacob Abbott
James Allen
James Andrews
James Baldwin
James Branch Cabell
James DeMille
James Joyce
James Lane Allen
James Lane Allen
James Oliver Curwood
James Oppenheim
James Otis
James R. Driscoll
Jane Austen
Jane L. Stewart
Janet Aldridge
Jens Peter Jacobsen
Jerome K. Jerome
John Burroughs
John Cournos
John F. Kennedy
John Gay
John Glasworthy

John Habberton
John Joy Bell
John Kendrick Bangs
John Milton
John Philip Sousa
Jonas Lauritz Idemil Lie
Jonathan Swift
Joseph A. Altsheler
Joseph Carey
Joseph Conrad
Joseph E. Badger Jr
Joseph Hergesheimer
Joseph Jacobs
Jules Vernes
Julian Hawthrone
Julie A Lippmann
Justin Huntly McCarthy
Kakuzo Okakura
Kenneth Grahame
Kenneth McGaffey
Kate Langley Bosher
Kate Langley Bosher
Katherine Cecil Thurston
Katherine Stokes
L. A. Abbot
L. T. Meade
L. Frank Baum
Latta Griswold
Laura Dent Crane
Laura Lee Hope
Laurence Housman
Lawrence Beasley
Leo Tolstoy
Leonid Andreyev
Lewis Carroll
Lewis Sperry Chafer
Lilian Bell
Lloyd Osbourne
Louis Hughes
Louis Tracy
Louisa May Alcott
Lucy Fitch Perkins
Lucy Maud Montgomery
Luther Benson
Lydia Miller Middleton
Lyndon Orr
M. Corvus
M. H. Adams
Margaret E. Sangster
Margret Howth
Margaret Vandercook

Margret Penrose
Maria Edgeworth
Maria Thompson Daviess
Mariano Azuela
Marion Polk Angellotti
Mark Overton
Mark Twain
Mary Austin
Mary Catherine Crowley
Mary Cole
Mary Hastings Bradley
Mary Roberts Rinehart
Mary Rowlandson
M. Wollstonecraft Shelley
Maud Lindsay
Max Beerbohm
Myra Kelly
Nathaniel Hawthrone
Nicolo Machiavelli
O. F. Walton
Oscar Wilde
Owen Johnson
P.G. Wodehouse
Paul and Mabel Thorne
Paul G. Tomlinson
Paul Severing
Percy Brebner
Peter B. Kyne
Plato
R. Derby Holmes
R. L. Stevenson
R. S. Ball
Rabindranath Tagore
Rahul Alvares
Ralph Bonehill
Ralph Henry Barbour
Ralph Victor
Ralph Waldo Emmerson
Rene Descartes
Rex Beach

Rex E. Beach
Richard Harding Davis
Richard Jefferies
Richard Le Gallienne
Robert Barr
Robert Frost
Robert Gordon Anderson
Robert L. Drake
Robert Lansing
Robert Lynd
Robert Michael Ballantyne
Robert W. Chambers
Rosa Nouchette Carey
Rudyard Kipling
Samuel B. Allison
Samuel Hopkins Adams
Sarah Bernhardt
Sarah C. Hallowell
Selma Lagerlof
Sherwood Anderson
Sigmund Freud
Standish O'Grady
Stanley Weyman
Stella Benson
Stella M. Francis
Stephen Crane
Stewart Edward White
Stijn Streuvels
Swami Abhedananda
Swami Parmananda
T. S. Ackland
T. S. Arthur
The Princess Der Ling
Thomas A. Janvier
Thomas A Kempis
Thomas Anderton
Thomas Bailey Aldrich
Thomas Bulfinch
Thomas De Quincey
Thomas Dixon

Thomas H. Huxley
Thomas Hardy
Thomas More
Thornton W. Burgess
U. S. Grant
Valentine Williams
Various Authors
Vaughan Kester
Victor Appleton
Victoria Cross
Virginia Woolf
Wadsworth Camp
Walter Camp
Walter Scott
Washington Irving
Wilbur Lawton
Wilkie Collins
Willa Cather
Willard F. Baker
William Dean Howells
William le Queux
W. Makepeace Thackeray
William W. Walter
William Shakespeare
Winston Churchill
Yei Theodora Ozaki
Yogi Ramacharaka
Young E. Allison
Zane Grey